Best
Garden Plants
for
Virginia

Richard N~~~~~~
Laura P~~~~

Lone Pine Publishing International

The Distributor: Lone Pine Publishing
1808 B Street NW, Suite 140
Auburn, WA, USA 98001
Website: www.lonepinepublishing.com

Library and Archives Canada Cataloguing in Publication

Nunnally, Richard, 1947–

   Best garden plants for Virginia / Richard Nunnally, Laura Peters.

Includes index.

ISBN–13: 978–976–8200–13–6
ISBN–10: 976–8200–13–8

   1. Plants, Ornamental--Virginia. 2. Gardening--Virginia.

I. Peters, Laura, 1968– II. Title.

SB453.2.V5N85 2006   635'.09755   C2005–906490–0

Scanning & Electronic Film: Elite Lithographers Co.

Front cover photographs by Tim Matheson and Tamara Eder except where noted. *Clockwise from top right:* Pat Austin rose, flowering crabapple, iris, lilac, amaryllis (*Laura Peters*), fringe tree, daylily (*Allison Penko*), lily (*Laura Peters*), tickseed, lily (*Erika Flatt*).

Photography: All photos by Tim Matheson, Tamara Eder and Laura Peters except:
AAFC 121b; Janet Davis 121a; Joan de Grey 36a; Don Doucette 104b; Jen Fafard 134a; Derek Fell 29a, 64a, 89, 112a, 126a, 137a&b, 138a, 141a, 142, 152b; Erika Flatt 9a, 136a; Saxon Holt 68a, 72a; Jackson & Perkins 115a&b; Kim O'Leary 70a, 93a, 96b, 133a, 147b; Colin Laroque 69b; Dawn Loewen 66a, 76a&b; Janet Loughrey 112b; 138b; Marilynn McAra 134b; Niche Gardens-Blair Durant 140a&b; Allison Penko 21b, 43a, 56a, 60b, 75a, 88b, 90b, 93b, 103b, 106a&b, 109a&b, 110b, 124b, 135a, 155a, 156a, 160a&b, 161, 164a, 165a&b; Photos.com 139a; Robert Ritchie 33b, 37a, 81a&b, 85a&b, 102a, 116a; Leila Sidi 139b; Peter Thompstone 55b; Mark Turner 128a, 141b, 152a; Don Williamson 131b, 132a&b; Tim Wood 86a.

This book is not intended as a 'how-to' guide for eating garden plants. No plant or plant extract should be consumed unless you are certain of its identity and toxicity and of your potential for allergic reactions.

PC: P13

Table of Contents

Introduction

Starting a garden can seem like a daunting task. Which plants should you choose? Where should you put them in the garden? This book is intended to give beginning gardeners the information they need to start planning and planting gardens of their own. It describes a wide variety of plants and provides basic planting information such as where and how to plant.

Virginia exhibits a wide diversity of ecological regions and each presents its own unique challenges. Each region has a temperature range that indicates relative hardiness. Consider this: 5° F is very different with snow cover or without; in soggy soil or in dry; following a hot summer or a long, cold, wet one. These factors will have more influence on the survival of plants than will temperature. Recognizing the type of climate in which you garden will help you determine hardiness. Your local garden center should be able to provide you with local hardiness zones and frost date information.

Hardiness zones and frost dates are two terms often used when discussing climate. Hardiness zones consider the temperatures and conditions in winter. Plants are rated based on the zones in which they grow successfully. The last frost date in spring combined with the first frost date in fall allows us to predict the length of the growing season.

Getting Started

When planning your garden, start with a quick analysis of the garden as it is now. Plants have different requirements and it is best to put the right plant in the right place rather than to change your garden to suit the plants you want.

Knowing which parts of your garden receive the most and least amounts of sunlight will help you choose the proper plants and decide where to plant them. Light is classified into four basic groups: full sun (direct, unobstructed light all or most of the day); partial shade (direct sun for about half the day and shade for the rest); light shade (shade all or most of the day with some sun filtering through to ground level); and full shade (no direct sunlight). Most plants prefer a specific amount of light, but many can adapt to a range of light levels.

Plants use the soil to hold themselves upright, but they also rely on the many resources it holds: air, water, nutrients, organic matter and a host of microbes. The particle size of the soil influences the amount of air, water and nutrients it can hold. Sand, with the largest particles, has a lot of air space and allows water and nutrients to drain quickly. Clay, with the smallest particles, is high in nutrients but has very little air space. Water is therefore slow to penetrate clay and slow to drain from it.

Soil acidity or alkalinity (measured on the pH scale) influences the nutrients available to plants. A pH of 7 is neutral; a lower pH is more acidic. Most plants prefer a soil with a pH of 5.5–7.5. Soil-testing kits are available at most garden centers, and soil samples can be sent to testing facilities for a more thorough analysis.

Compost is one of the best and most important amendments you can add to any type of soil. Compost improves soil by adding organic matter and nutrients, introducing soil microbes, increasing water retention and improving drainage. Compost can be purchased, or you can make it in your own backyard.

Microclimates are small areas that are generally warmer or colder than the surrounding area. Buildings, fences, trees and other large structures can provide extra shelter in winter, but may trap heat in summer, thus creating a warmer microclimate. The bottoms of hills are usually colder than the tops, but may not be as windy. Take advantage of these areas when you plan your garden and choose your plants; you may even grow out-of-zone plants successfully in a warm, sheltered location.

Hardiness Zones Map

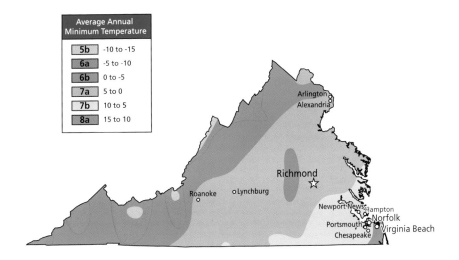

Average Annual Minimum Temperature	
5b	-10 to -15
6a	-5 to -10
6b	0 to -5
7a	5 to 0
7b	10 to 5
8a	15 to 10

Selecting Plants

It's important to purchase healthy plants that are free of pests and diseases. Such plants will establish quickly in your garden and won't introduce problems that may spread to other plants. You should have a good idea of what the plant is supposed to look like—the color and shape of the leaves and the habit of the plant—and then inspect the plant for signs of disease or infestation.

The majority of plants are container grown. This is an efficient way for nurseries and greenhouses to grow plants, but when plants grow in a restricted space for too long, they can become pot bound with their roots densely encircling the inside of the pot. Avoid purchasing plants in this condition; they are often stressed and can take longer to establish. In some cases they may not establish at all. If you find yourself with root bound plants, be sure to pry the roots apart before planting. This will help them to become established in your garden. It is often possible to remove pots temporarily to look at the condition of the roots. You can check for soil-borne insects and rotten roots at the same time.

Planting Basics

The following tips apply to all plants:

- Prepare the garden before planting. Dig over the soil, pull up any weeds and make any needed amendments before you begin planting, if possible.

This may be more difficult in established beds to which you want to add a single plant. The prepared area should be at least twice the size of the plant you want to put in and preferably the expected size of the mature plant.

- Settle the soil with water. Good contact between the roots and the soil is important, but if you press the soil down too firmly, as often happens when you step on the soil, you can cause compaction, which reduces the movement of water through the soil and leaves very few air spaces. Instead, pour water in as you fill the hole with soil. The water will settle the soil evenly without allowing it to compact.

- Unwrap the roots. It is always best to remove any container before planting to give roots the chance to spread out naturally when planted. In particular, you should remove plastic containers, fiber pots, wire and burlap before planting trees. Fiber pots decompose very slowly, if at all, and wick moisture away from the plant. Synthetic burlap won't decompose, and wire can strangle the roots as they mature. The only exceptions to this rule are peat pots and pellets used to start annuals and vegetables; these decompose and can be planted with the young transplants.

- Accommodate the rootball. Dig the hole two to three times the width of the rootball. The hole should be no

Gently remove container. Ensure proper planting depth. Backfill with soil.

deeper than the height of the rootball. The top of the rootball should be level with the surrounding ground. It's important not to plant it too deeply.

- Know the mature size. Place your plants based on how big the plants will grow rather than how big they are when you plant them. Large plants should have enough room to mature without interfering with walls, roof overhangs, power lines and walkways.

- Plant at the same depth in the soil. Plants generally like to grow at a certain level in relation to the soil and should be planted at the same level they were growing at before you transplanted them.

- Identify your plants. Keep track of what's what in your garden by putting a tag next to your plant when you plant it, or by making an overhead drawing with plant names and locations. It is very easy for beginning gardeners to forget exactly what they planted and where they planted it.

- Water deeply and infrequently. It's better to water deeply once every week or two rather than to water lightly more often. Deep watering forces roots to grow as they search for water and helps them survive dry spells when water bans may restrict your watering regime. Always check the rootzone before you water. More gardeners overwater than underwater.

Annuals

Annuals are only expected to last for a single growing season. Their flowers and decorative foliage provide bright splashes of color and can fill in spaces around immature trees, shrubs and perennials.

Annuals are easy to plant and are usually sold in small packs of four or six. The roots quickly fill the space in these small packs, so the small rootball should be broken up before planting. Split the ball in two up the center, or run your thumb up each side to break up the roots.

Many annuals are grown from seed and can be started directly in the garden. Plants that dislike having their roots disturbed are often grown directly from seed or grown in peat pots or pellets to minimize root disturbance.

Winter annuals can be planted in late fall and early winter. Summer annuals can be planted in spring. Be aware of your local frost dates, as some summer annuals are quite tender.

Perennials

Perennials grow for three or more years. They usually die back to the ground each fall and send up new shoots in spring, though some are evergreen. They often have a shorter period of bloom than annuals but require less care.

Many perennials benefit from being divided every few years. This keeps them

Settle backfilled soil with water.

Water the plant well.

Add a layer of mulch.

growing and blooming vigorously, and in some cases controls their spread. Dividing involves digging the plant up, removing dead bits, breaking the plant into several pieces and replanting some or all of the pieces. Extra pieces can be given as gifts to family, friends and neighbors.

Trees & Shrubs

Trees and shrubs provide the bones of the garden. They are often the slowest growing plants but usually live the longest. Characterized by leaf type, they may be deciduous or evergreen, and needled or broad-leaved.

Trees should have as little disturbed soil as possible at the bottom of the planting hole. Loose dirt settles over time and sinking even an inch can kill some trees.

Staking, sometimes recommended for newly planted trees, is only necessary for trees over 5' tall.

Pruning is more often required for shrubs than trees. It helps them maintain an attractive shape and can improve blooming. It is a good idea to take a pruning course or to hire or consult with an ISA (International Society of Arboriculture) certified arborist if you have never pruned before.

Roses are lovely on their own or in mixed borders.

Roses

Roses are beautiful shrubs with lovely, often-fragrant, blooms. Traditionally, most roses only bloomed once in the growing season, but new varieties bloom all, or almost all, summer.

Generally, roses prefer a fertile, well-prepared planting area. A rule of thumb is to prepare a circular area 24" in diameter and 24" deep. Add plenty of compost or other fertile organic matter and keep roses well watered during the growing season. Many roses are quite durable and will adapt to poorer conditions. Roses, like all shrubs, have specific pruning requirements.

Vines

Vines or climbing plants are useful for screening and shade, especially in a location too small for a tree. They may be woody or herbaceous and annual or perennial.

Most vines need sturdy supports to grow up on. Trellises, arbors, porch railings, fences, walls, poles and trees are all possible supports. If a support is needed, ensure it's in place before you plant to avoid disturbing the roots later.

Trees and shrubs provide backbone to your landscape.

Training vines to climb arbors adds structure to the garden.

Lilies bloom throughout the summer.

Basically any plant that covers the ground can be used as a groundcover. Groundcovers are often spreading plants with dense growth that are used to control soil erosion, to keep weeds at bay and to fill garden areas that are difficult to maintain. Groundcovers can be herbaceous or woody and annual or perennial.

Vines and plants that are aggressive spreaders make excellent groundcovers, but any plant with dense growth, if enough of them are planted, will serve the purpose. Space plants closer together when planting to ensure the ground is completely covered.

Bulbs

These plants have fleshy, underground storage organs that allow them to survive extended periods of dormancy. They are often grown for the bright splashes of color their flowers provide. They may be spring, summer or fall flowering.

Hardy bulbs can be left in the ground and will flower every year, but many popular, tender plants grow from bulbs, corms or tubers. These tender plants are generally lifted from the garden in fall as the foliage dies back and are stored in a cool, frost-free location for winter, to be replanted in spring.

Herbs

Herbs may be medicinal or culinary and are often both. A few common culinary herbs are listed in this book. Even if you don't cook with herbs, the often-fragrant foliage adds its aroma to the garden, and the plants have decorative forms, leaves and flowers.

Many herbs have pollen-producing flowers that attract butterflies, bees and hummingbirds to the garden. They also attract predatory insects. These useful insects help to manage your pest problems by feasting on problem insects such as aphids, mealy bugs and whiteflies.

Foliage Plants

Foliage is an important consideration when choosing plants for your garden. Although many plants look spectacular in bloom, they can seem rather dull without flowers. Including a variety of plants with unique, interesting or striking foliage in your garden can provide all the color and texture you want without the need to rely on flowers.

Many herbs grow well in pots and planters.

Ornamental grasses are becoming very popular additions to the garden. Grasses offer a variety of textures and foliage colors, and at least three seasons of interest. There is an ornamental grass for every garden situation and condition. Some grasses will thrive in any garden condition, including hot and dry to cool and wet, and in all types of soils.

Foliage plants add color, variety and texture.

Ornamental grasses have very few insect or disease problems. They require very little maintenance other than cutting the perennial grasses back in fall or spring. If you plan to leave dried grass standing for winter interest, be aware that it can present a fire hazard. Dry grass is highly flammable and should be cut back in fall if it is near a house or other structure.

Ferns are ancient plants that have adapted to many different environments. The fern family is a very large group of plants with interesting foliage in a wide array of shapes and colors. Ferns do not produce flowers, but instead reproduce by spores borne in structures on the undersides and margins of the foliage. Ferns are generally planted in moist, shaded gardens, but some will thrive in dry shade under the deep shade of some trees, such as magnolia.

Throughout the book, we have included a variety of plants grown for their foliage. Many annuals, perennials, trees, shrubs, vines and herbs have wonderful foliage, and they will be an asset to your garden landscape.

Final Comments

We encourage you to visit the outstanding garden shows, county fairs, public gardens, arboretums and private gardens (get permission first) we have here in Virginia to see what plants grow best and to see if any plants catch your interest. A walk through your neighborhood is also a grand way to see what plants might do well in your own garden. Don't be afraid to ask questions.

Also, don't be afraid to experiment. No matter how many books you read, trying things yourself is the best way to learn and to find out what will grow in your garden. Use the information provided as guidelines, and have fun!

Ageratum
Ageratum

A. houstonianum 'Blue Horizon' (above), *A. houstonianum* (below)

The fluffy flowers, often in shades of blue, add softness and texture to the garden.

Growing
Ageratum prefers **full sun** but tolerates partial shade. The soil should be **fertile, moist** and **well drained**. A moisture-retaining mulch will prevent the soil from drying out excessively. Deadhead to prolong blooming and to keep plants looking tidy.

Tips
The smaller selections, which become almost completely covered in flowers, make excellent edging plants for flowerbeds and are attractive when grouped in masses or grown in planters. The taller selections can be included in the center of a flowerbed and are useful as cut flowers.

Recommended
A. houstonianum forms a large, leggy mound that can grow up to 24" tall, though many cultivars have been developed that have a low, bushy habit and generally grow about 12" tall. Flowers are produced in shades of blue, purple, pink or white.

The genus name, Ageratum, *is from the Greek, meaning 'without age,' and refers to the long-lasting flowers.*

Features: fuzzy blue, purple, pink, white flowers; mounded habit **Height:** 6–36"
Spread: 6–18"

Begonia
Begonia

B. Rex Cultorum Hybrid 'Escargot' (above)
B. x *tuberhybrida* (below)

Water along the edge of containers or around the dripline of in-ground tuberous begonias to prevent tuber rot— never water near the stem. Keep the mildew-prone foliage dry.

Whether you want beautiful flowers, a compact habit or decorative foliage, there is a begonia to fulfill your shade gardening needs.

Growing

Begonias prefer **light to partial shade** and **fertile, neutral to acidic, well-drained** soil with a lot of **organic matter**. Some wax begonias tolerate sun if their soil is kept moist. Allow the soil to dry out slightly between waterings, particularly for tuberous begonias. Plant begonias in warm soil. In cold soil, they may become stunted and fail to thrive.

Tips

Plant trailing tuberous begonias in hanging baskets and along rock walls. Wax begonias make attractive edging plants. Rex begonias are useful as specimen plants in containers and beds.

Recommended

B. Rex Cultorum Hybrids (rex begonias) are grown for their dramatic, colorful foliage.

B. semperflorens (wax begonias) have pink, white, red or bicolored flowers, a neat, rounded habit and green, bronze, reddish or white-variegated foliage.

B. x *tuberhybrida* (tuberous begonias) are generally sold as tubers. Their flowers bloom in many shades of red, pink, yellow, orange or white.

Features: pink, white, red, yellow, orange, bicolored, picotee flowers; decorative foliage
Height: 6–24" **Spread:** 6–24"

Celosia
Celosia

$\mathcal{T}$he unusual wrinkled texture of the flowers and the incredible variety of flower forms of celosia will make any gardener crow with delight.

Growing
A **sheltered** spot in **full sun** is best. The soil should be **fertile** and **well drained** with plenty of **organic material** worked in. Celosias like to be watered regularly.

It is preferable to start celosias directly in the garden. If you need to start them indoors, start the seeds in peat pots or pellets and plant them in the garden before they begin to flower. If left too long in the pots, the plants will have stunted growth and won't be able to adapt to the garden. Keep seeds moist while they are germinating, and do not cover them.

Tips
Use celosia in borders and beds as well as in planters. The flowers make interesting additions to cut arrangements, either fresh or dried. A mass planting of plume celosia looks bright and cheerful in the garden. The popular crested varieties work well as accents and as cut flowers.

Recommended
C. argentea is the species from which both the crested and plume-type cultivars have been developed. The species itself is never grown. **Cristata Group** (crested celosia) has blooms that resemble brains or rooster combs. This group has many varieties and cultivars in bright, vivid colors. **Plumosa Group** (plume celosia) has feathery, plume-like blooms. This group also has many varieties and cultivars in deep, rich colors.

Features: red, orange, gold, yellow, pink, purple flowers **Height:** 10–36" **Spread:** 10–36"

C. argentea Plumosa Group (above)
C. argentea Cristata Group (below)

To dry the plumes, pick the flowers when they are at their peak and hang them upside down in a cool, shaded place.

Coleus
Solenostemon (Coleus)

S. scutellarioides cultivars (above & below)

Coleus can be trained to grow into a standard (tree) form by pinching off the side branches as the plant grows. Once the plant reaches the desired height, pinch from the top.

There is a coleus for everyone. With foliage from brash yellows, oranges and reds to deep maroon and rose, the colors, textures and variations of coleus are almost limitless.

Growing
Coleus prefers to grow in **light or partial shade**, but it tolerates full shade if the shade isn't too dense, or full sun if the plants are watered regularly. The soil should be of **rich to average fertility, humus rich, moist** and **well drained**.

Tips
The bold, colorful foliage makes a dramatic impact when the plants are grouped together as edging plants or in beds, borders or mixed containers. Coleus can also be grown indoors as a houseplant in a bright room.

When flower buds develop, it is best to pinch them off, because the plants tend to stretch out and become less attractive after they flower.

Recommended
S. scutellarioides (*Coleus blumei* var. *verschaffeltii*) forms a bushy mound of foliage. The leaf edges range from slightly toothed to very ruffled. The leaves are usually multi-colored with shades ranging from pale greenish yellow to deep purple-black. Dozens of cultivars are available, but many cannot be started from seed. **Sunlover Series** is a sun-loving group of coleus available in wonderful color combinations.

Features: brightly colored foliage; insignificant purple flowers **Height:** 6–36" **Spread:** usually equal to height

Dusty Miller

Senecio

S. *cineraria* 'Silver Dust' (above), S. *cinerara* (below)

Dusty miller makes a great addition to planters, window boxes and mixed borders where the soft, silvery gray, deeply-lobed foliage makes a good backdrop for the brightly-colored flowers of other annuals.

Growing

Dusty miller grows well in **full sun to partial shade**. The soil should be of **average fertility** and **well drained**.

Tips

The soft, silvery, lacy foliage of this plant is its main feature. Dusty miller is used primarily as an edging plant, but also in beds, borders and containers.

Pinch off the flowers before they bloom. They aren't showy and they steal energy that would otherwise go to producing more foliage.

Dusty miller is a subshrub that is used as an annual.

Recommended

S. cineraria forms a mound of fuzzy, silvery gray, lobed or finely divided foliage. Many cultivars with impressive foliage colors and shapes have been developed.

When cut for fresh or dried-flower arrangements, dusty miller makes a wonderful filler that adds a lacy texture.

Features: silvery foliage; neat habit; yellow to cream flowers **Height:** 12–24" **Spread:** equal to height or slightly narrower

Geranium
Pelargonium

P. peltatum (above & below)

The name Pelargonium *arises from the Greek word 'pelargos,' which means stork, and refers to the similarity between a stork's bill and the shape of the fruit.*

Geraniums have earned their respected place in the annual garden, but be sure to buy plants that can take the heat and humidity.

Growing
Geraniums perform best in **morning sun and afternoon shade**. The soil should be **fertile** and **well drained**. Deadheading is essential to keep geraniums blooming and looking neat. Geraniums can be damaged by heavy rains.

Tips
Geraniums are popular for use in borders, beds, planters, hanging baskets and window boxes.

Recommended
P. x *domesticum* (regal geranium, Martha Washington geranium) has heart-shaped foliage and larger, frillier flowers than other geraniums. It works best in containers and tends not to perform well in gardens. It does not tolerate heat as well as do other varieties.

P. x *hortorum* (zonal geranium) is a bushy plant with red, pink, purple, orange or white flowers and, frequently, banded or multi-colored foliage.

P. peltatum (ivy-leaved geranium) has thick, waxy leaves and a trailing habit. It is one of the best plants to include in a mixed hanging basket.

P. **species and cultivars** (scented geraniums) have fragrant and often decorative foliage. The scents are grouped into the categories of rose, mint, citrus, fruit, spice or pungent.

Features: red, pink, violet, orange, salmon, white, purple flowers; decorative or scented foliage; variable habits **Height:** 8–24" **Spread:** 6"–4'

Gerbera Daisy

Gerbera

G. jamesonii (above & below)

Most gardeners associate this flower with nothing other than fresh flower arrangements, but it is also a fine bedding plant and annual performer in the garden and in containers.

Growing

Gerbera daisy prefers **full sun** but tolerates partial shade. The soil should be **well drained**, have plenty of **organic matter** and be of **average to high fertility**. To keep the crown of the plant dry, set the crown just above the soil line. If your soil is poorly drained, use a raised bed. Allow the soil to almost dry out between waterings.

Tips

Gerbera daisy makes an impressive addition to annual beds and borders, as well as to mixed or solo containers.

Gerbera daisy is popular as a cut flower. For longer-lasting flowers, slit the stem bottoms one inch to help them absorb water. Cut the stems under warm water for maximum water saturation.

Recommended

G. jamesonii is a clump-forming plant. Yellow-centered flowers in solid shades of yellow, orange, apricot or red bloom from late spring to late summer. Many cultivars are available in a wide variety of colors.

Gerbera daisy is also used as a short-lived houseplant.

Features: colorful, large, daisy-like flowers
Height: 12–18" **Spread:** 24"

Impatiens
Impatiens

I. walleriana (above), *I. hawkeri* (below)

Impatiens are the high-wattage dar-lings of the shade garden, delivering masses of flowers in a wide variety of colors.

Growing
Impatiens do best in **partial shade** or **light shade** but tolerate full shade or, if kept moist, full sun. New Guinea impa-tiens are the best adapted to sunny loca-tions. The soil should be **fertile, humus rich, moist** and **well drained**.

Tips
Impatiens are known for their ability to grow and flower profusely, even in shade. Mass plant them in beds under trees, along shady fences and walls or in porch planters. They also look lovely in hanging baskets. New Guinea impatiens are grown as much for their variegated leaves as for their flowers.

Recommended
I. hawkeri (New Guinea hybrids, New Guinea impatiens) flowers in shades of red, orange, pink, purple or white. The foliage is often variegated with a yellow stripe down the center of each leaf. Many cultivars are available in various flower and foliage colors.

I. walleriana (impatiens, busy Lizzie) flowers in shades of purple, red, bur-gundy, pink, yellow, salmon, orange, apricot or white and can be bicolored. Dozens of cultivars are available.

Features: flowers in hues of purple, red, burgundy, pink, yellow, salmon, orange, apricot, white, bicolored; flowers well in shade
Height: 6–36" **Spread:** 12–24"

Lobelia
Lobelia

Lobelia is a lovely plant that adds color to shady spots and blends well with fuchsias and begonias. Luckily, lobelia also does well in the sun. Lobelias and marigolds make a striking combination.

Growing
Lobelia grows well in **full sun** or **partial shade**, in **fertile, moist, fairly well-drained** soil high in **organic matter**. Lobelia likes cool summer nights. Ensure that the soil stays moist in hot weather. Plant out after the last frost.

Because seedlings are prone to damping off, be sure to use a good, clean, seed-starting soil mix. Damping off causes the plants to rot at the soil level, flop over and die.

Tips
Use lobelia along the edges of beds and borders, on rock walls, and in rock gardens, mixed containers and hanging baskets.

Trim lobelia back after its first wave of flowers. This helps ensure the plant flowers through summer. In hot areas, lobelia may die back over summer but usually revives as the weather cools.

Recommended
L. erinus may be rounded and bushy, or low and trailing. Many cultivars are available in both of these forms.

L. erinus 'Sapphire' (above), *L. erinus* cultivar (below)

Lobelia *was named after the Flemish physician and botanist Mathias de l'Obel (1538–1616).*

Features: abundant purple, blue, pink, white, red flowers **Height:** 3–9"
Spread: 6" or wider

Marigold
Tagetes

T. patula Boy Series (above), *T. patula* cultivar (below)

Slugs really enjoy the marigold's scented foliage—be sure to protect your plants from these creatures.

From the large, exotic, ruffled flowers of African marigold to the tiny flowers on the low-growing signet marigold, the warm colors and fresh scent of marigolds add a festive air to the garden.

Growing

Marigolds grow best in **full sun**. The soil should be of **average fertility** and **well drained**. These plants are drought tolerant and hold up well in windy, rainy weather. However, too much water may cause rot. Minimize overhead watering. Sow seeds directly in the garden after the chance of frost has passed. Deadhead to prolong blooming and to keep plants tidy.

Tips

Mass planted or mixed with other plants, marigolds make a vibrant addition to beds, borders and container gardens. These plants will thrive in the hottest, driest parts of your garden.

Recommended

T. erecta (African marigold, American marigold, Aztec marigold) is the largest plant with the biggest flowers.

T. patula (French marigold) is low growing and has a wide range of flower colors.

T. tenuifolia (signet marigold) has feathery foliage and small, dainty flowers.

T. **Triploid hybrids** have huge flowers and compact growth.

Features: yellow, red, orange, brown, gold, cream, bicolored flowers; fragrant foliage; easy to grow **Height:** 6–36" **Spread:** 12–24"

Ornamental Kale

Brassica

Ornamental kale has stunning, variegated foliage and is wonderful in containers and flower boxes.

Growing

Ornamental kale prefers **full sun** but tolerates partial shade. The soil should be **neutral to slightly alkaline, fertile, well drained** and **moist**. For best results, fertilize a couple of times through the winter.

Ornamental kale plants can be started in trays and transplanted in fall. Many packages of seeds contain a variety of cultivars.

The plant colors brighten after a light frost or when the air temperature drops below 50° F.

Tips

Ornamental kale is a tough, bold plant that is at home in both vegetable gardens and flowerbeds.

Wait until some true leaves develop before thinning. When thinning seedlings, use those that are not transplanted in salads.

Recommended

B. oleracea (**Acephala Group**) forms loose, erect rosettes of large, often fringed leaves in shades of purple, red, pink or white. It grows 12–24" tall with an equal spread. **Osaka Series** grows 12" tall and wide, with wavy foliage that is red to pink in the center and blue to green to the outside.

B. oleracea cultivars (above & below)

When ornamental kale bolts (sends up flowers), it is best to remove the flowers to extend the ornamental value of the plant.

Features: colorful, edible foliage
Height: 12–24" **Spread:** 12–24"

Pansy
Viola

V. x wittrockiana cultivars (above), *V. tricolor* (below)

Pansies are one of the most popular annuals available, and for good reason. They're often planted in early spring, long before any other annual, because they tolerate frost like no other. They continue to bloom and bloom, with little care.

Growing

Pansies prefer **full sun** but tolerate partial shade. The soil should be **fertile**, **moist** and **well drained**. Pansies do best in cool weather.

Tips

Pansies can be used in beds and borders or mixed with spring-flowering bulbs. They can also be grown in containers. With the varied color combinations

The more flowers you pick, the more profusely the plants will bloom, so deadhead throughout the summer months.

available, pansies complement almost every other type of bedding plant.

Plant a second crop of pansies late in summer to refresh tired flowerbeds well into the cool months of fall. Pansies will often reawaken in spring if left to go dormant in fall, allowing for early spring blooms that aren't afraid of a little late frost.

Recommended

V. tricolor (Johnny jump up) is a perennial grown as an annual. It bears flowers in shades of purple, lavender blue, white or yellow, with dark purple, upper petals. The lower petals are usually streaked with dark purple. Many cultivars exist with larger flowers and in various colors.

V. x wittrockiana is available in a wide variety of solid, patterned, bicolored or multi-colored flowers with face-like markings in every size imaginable. The foliage is bright green and lightly scalloped along the edges.

Features: blue, purple, red, orange, yellow, pink, white, multi-colored flowers
Height: 3–10" **Spread:** 6–12"

Petunia

Petunia

Milliflora type 'Fantasy' (above), Multiflora type (below)

For speedy growth, prolific blooming, ease of care and a huge variety of selections, petunias are hard to beat.

Growing

Petunias prefer **full sun**. The soil should be of **average to rich fertility, light, sandy** and **well drained**. Pinch halfway back in mid-summer to keep plants bushy and to encourage new growth and flowers.

Tips

Use petunias in beds, borders, containers and hanging baskets.

Recommended

P. x *hybrida* is a large group of popular, sun-loving annuals that fall into three categories: **grandifloras** have the largest flowers in the widest range of colors, but they can be damaged by rain; **multifloras** bear more flowers that are smaller and less easily damaged by heavy rain; and **millifloras** have the smallest flowers in the narrowest range of colors, but this type is the most prolific and least likely to be damaged by heavy rain. Cultivars of all types are available and new selections are made available almost every year.

The rekindling of interest in petunias was largely owing to the development of exciting new selections, such as the Supertunia hybrids and Wave family of petunias. These hybrid series are continuous-blooming, vigorous-spreading, dense-growing, wet-weather-tolerant plants that offer tremendous options for hanging baskets, containers and borders.

Features: flowers in every color, solid, bicolored, multi-colored; versatile plants
Height: 6–18" **Spread:** 12–24" or wider

Rock Rose

Portulaca

P. grandiflora (above & below)

These plants can be placed close together and allowed to intertwine for an interesting and attractive effect.

For a brilliant show in the hottest, driest, most neglected area of the garden, you can't go wrong with rock rose.

Growing

Rock rose requires **full sun**. The soil should be of **poor fertility, sandy** and **well drained**. To ensure that you will have plants where you want them, start seeds indoors. If you sow directly outdoors, the tiny seeds may get washed away by rain, and the plants will pop up in unexpected places. Rock rose also self-seeds and can provide a colorful show from year to year.

Tips

Rock rose grows well under the eaves of a house or in a dry, rocky, exposed area. It also makes a great addition to a hanging basket on a sunny front porch. Remember to water it occasionally. As long as the location is sunny, this plant will do well with minimal care.

Recommended

P. grandiflora forms a bushy mound of succulent foliage. It bears delicate, papery, rose-like flowers profusely all summer. Many cultivars are available, including those with flowers that stay open on cloudy days.

Features: colorful, drought-resistant summer flowers in shades of red, pink, yellow, white, purple, orange, peach **Height:** 4–8"
Spread: 6–12" or wider

Salvia

Salvia

Salvias should be part of every annual garden—the attractive and varied forms have something to offer every style of garden.

Growing

All salvia plants prefer **full sun** but tolerate light shade. The soil should be **moist** and **well drained** and of **average to rich fertility**, with a lot of **organic matter**.

Tips

Salvias look good grouped in beds and borders and in containers. The flowers are long lasting and make good cut flowers for arrangements.

To keep plants producing flowers, water them often and fertilize monthly.

Recommended

S. argentea (silver sage) is grown for its large, fuzzy, silvery leaves. *S. coccinea* (Texas sage) is a bushy, upright plant that bears whorled spikes of white, pink, blue or purple flowers. *S. farinacea* (mealy cup sage, blue sage) has bright blue flowers clustered along stems powdered with silver. Cultivars are available. *S. splendens* (salvia, scarlet sage) is grown for its spikes of bright red, tubular flowers. Recently, cultivars have become available in white, pink, purple or orange. *S. viridis* (*S. horminium*; annual clary sage) is grown for its colorful pink, purple, blue or white bracts, not for its flowers.

S. splendens (above), *S. viridis* (below)

With over 900 species of Salvia, *you're sure to find one you'll like for your garden.*

Features: red, blue, purple, burgundy, pink, orange, salmon, yellow, cream, white, bicolored summer flowers; attractive foliage
Height: 8–48" **Spread:** 8–48"

Snapdragon
Antirrhinum

A. majus cultivars (above & below)

Snapdragons are among the most appealing plants. The flower colors are always rich and vibrant, and even the most jaded gardeners are tempted to squeeze open the dragons' mouths.

Growing
Snapdragons prefer **full sun** but tolerate light or partial shade. The soil should be **fertile, humus rich, neutral to alkaline** and **well drained**. These plants do not perform well in acidic soil. Do not cover the seeds when sowing because they require light for germination.

Snapdragons may survive the winter, but they grow best when they're planted annually.

To encourage bushy growth, pinch the tips of the young plants. Cut off the flower spikes as they fade to promote further blooming and to prevent the plant from dying back before the end of the season.

Tips
The height of the variety dictates the best place for it in a border—the shortest varieties work well near the front, and the tallest look good in the back. The dwarf and medium-height varieties can be used in planters. The trailing varieties do well in hanging baskets.

Recommended
There are many cultivars of **A. majus** available. They are generally grouped into three size categories: dwarf, medium and giant.

Features: white, cream, yellow, orange, red, maroon, pink, purple, bicolored summer flowers
Height: 6"–4' **Spread:** 6–24"

Sunflower

Helianthus

The image of sunflowers along a weathered barn or tall garden shed has inspired artists of all ages throughout history.

Growing

Sunflowers grow best in **full sun**. The soil should be of **average fertility, humus rich, moist** and **well drained**.

The annual sunflower is an excellent plant for children to grow. The seeds are big and easy to handle, and they germinate quickly. The plant's upward growth can be measured until the flower finally appears on top.

Tips

The lower-growing varieties can be used in beds and borders. The tall varieties are effective at the back of borders and make good screens and temporary hedges. The tallest varieties may need staking.

Carefree gardeners let sunflowers go to seed right in the garden to produce new blooms the following summer.

Recommended

H. annuus (common sunflower) is considered weedy, but many attractive new cultivars have been developed.

H. annuus 'Teddy Bear' (above), *H. annuus* cultivar (below)

Birds will flock to the ripening seedheads of your sunflowers and quickly pluck out the tightly packed seeds.

Features: most commonly yellow, but also orange, red, brown, cream or bicolored flowers; typically with brown, purple or rusty red centers; edible seeds **Height:** dwarf varieties 24"; giants up to 15' **Spread:** 12–24"

Sweet Alyssum
Lobularia

L. maritima (above & below)

Leave alyssum plants out all winter. In spring, remove the previous year's growth to expose the self-sown seedlings below.

Sweet alyssum makes a lovely carpet of blooms to weave through formal and informal plantings. It is excellent for creating soft edges in beds and borders and along pathways.

Growing
Sweet alyssum prefers **full sun** but tolerates light shade. **Well-drained** soil of **average fertility** is preferred, but poor soil is tolerated. Sweet alyssum may die back a bit during hot and humid summers. Trim it back and water it periodically to encourage new growth and more flowers when the weather cools.

Tips
Sweet alyssum creeps around rock gardens, over rock walls and along the edges of beds. It is an excellent choice for seeding into cracks and crevices of walkways and between patio stones. Once established it readily reseeds. It is also good for filling in spaces between tall plants in borders and mixed containers.

Recommended
L. maritima forms a low, spreading mound of foliage. The entire plant appears to be covered in tiny blossoms when in full flower. Cultivars are available in a wide range of flower colors, including **'Wonderland'** that bears rosy-red blossoms.

Features: fragrant, pink, purple, yellow, salmon, white flowers **Height:** 3–12"
Spread: 6–24"

Sweet William
Dianthus

D. barbatus mixed cultivars (above), cultivar (below)

Sweet william has been a favorite bedding plant for generations. It tolerates pollution, making it a good choice for small urban gardens.

Growing
Sweet william prefers **full sun** but tolerates some light shade. Keep this plant **sheltered** from strong winds and the hottest afternoon sun. A **light, neutral** or **alkaline, humus-rich, well-drained** soil is preferred. The most important factor in the successful cultivation of sweet william is drainage.

Tips
Sweet william is great for mass planting and for edging flower borders and walkways. Use these plants in the rock garden, or try them as cut flowers.

Recommended
D. barbatus is a biennial mostly grown as an annual. It grows 18–24" tall and

spreads 8–12". Flattened clusters of two-toned white, pink, red or purple-red flowers bloom in late spring to early summer. **'Indian Carpet Mix'** is a dwarf, compact selection with flowers in a wide array of colors but mostly in shades of pink. The **Roundabout Series** grows approximately 8–12" tall and produces solid or two-toned blooms in the first year from seed.

The genus name, Dianthus, *is a combination of 'Dios' (a form of the name Zeus) and 'anthos' (flower), so it means 'flower of the gods.'*

Features: colorful, two-toned flowers; habit
Height: 8–24" **Spread:** 8–12

Zinnia

Zinnia

Z. angustifolia 'Profusion White' (above)
Z. elegans cultivars (below)

*Z*innias are popular in gardens and flower arrangements, adding much needed color to the late-summer and fall garden.

Growing

Grow zinnias in **full sun.** The soil should be **fertile, rich in organic matter, moist** and **well drained.** To avoid disturbing the roots when transplanting seedlings, start the seeds in individual peat pots. Deadhead to prolong blooming and to keep plants looking neat.

Tips

Zinnias are useful in beds, borders, containers and cutting gardens. The dwarf selections can be used as edging plants. Zinnias provide wonderful fall color.

Recommended

Z. angustifolia (spreading zinnia, narrowleaf zinnia) is a low, mounding, mildewresistant plant that bears yellow, orange or white flowers. It grows to about 8" tall. Cultivars are available, including the **Profusion Series,** which bears flowers in shades of pink, orange or white.

Z. elegans (common zinnia) is a bushy, upright plant with daisy-like flowers in a variety of forms. Heights vary from 6–36". Many cultivars are available, including selections from different subgroups with flowers of varied forms. These forms include double, cactus flowers with quilled petals and crested flowers with rounded, cushion-like centers surrounded by wide petals. All forms are available in a wide variety of colors and sizes.

Z. haageana (Mexican zinnia) is a bushy plant with narrow leaves that bears bright bicolored or tricolored, daisy-like flowers in shades of orange, red, yellow, maroon, brown or gold. Plants grow 12–24" tall. Cultivars are available.

Features: bushy plants; flowers in shades of red, yellow, green, purple, orange, pink, white, maroon, brown, gold, some are bicolored or tricolored **Height:** 6–36" **Spread:** 12"

Aster

Aster (Symphyotrichum)

A sters are among the final plants to bloom before the snow flies; their purples and pinks contrast with the yellow-flowered perennials common in the late-summer and fall garden.

Growing

Asters prefer **full sun** but tolerate partial shade. The soil should be **fertile, moist** and **well drained**. Pinch or shear these plants back in early summer to promote dense growth and to reduce disease problems. Mulch in winter to protect plants from temperature fluctuations. Divide asters every two or three years to maintain vigor and control spread.

Tips

Use asters in the middle of borders and in cottage gardens, or naturalize them in wild gardens.

Recommended

Some *Aster* species have recently been reclassified under the genus *Symphyotrichum*. You may see both names at garden centers.

A. x *frikartii* (frikart aster) is an upright perennial with dark green, roughly textured leaves and light to dark violet blue flowers that emerge in late summer. This selection grows 2–3' tall and wide. Cultivars are available with lavender and blue flowers.

A. novae-angliae (Michaelmas daisy, New England aster) is an upright,

A. novae-angliae (above), A. novi-belgii (below)

spreading, clump-forming perennial that bears yellow-centered, purple flowers. Many cultivars are available.

A. novi-belgii (Michaelmas daisy, New York aster) is a dense, upright, clump-forming perennial with purple flowers. Many cultivars are available.

Features: late-summer to mid-autumn flowers in shades of red, white, blue, purple, pink, often with yellow centers **Height:** 10–60" **Spread:** 18–36" **Hardiness:** zones 3–8

Astilbe

Astilbe

A. x arendsii cultivars (above)
A. x arendsii 'Bressingham Beauty' (below)

Astilbes are beacons in the shade. Their high-impact flowers will brighten any gloomy area of your garden.

In late summer, transplant seedlings found near the parent plant to create plumes of color all through the garden.

Growing

Astilbes grow best in **light** or **partial shade** but tolerate full shade, though they will not flower as much. The soil should be **fertile, humus rich, acidic, moist** and **well drained**. Astilbes appreciate moist soil, but not standing water.

Divide astilbe every three years or so to maintain plant vigor. If maturing root masses lift out of the soil, add a layer of topsoil and mulch.

Tips

Grow astilbes near the edges of bog gardens and ponds and in woodland gardens and shaded borders.

Recommended

There are many species, hybrids and cultivars of astilbe available. In general, these plants form bushy clumps of leaves and bear plumes of colorful flowers. The following are a few popular selections. **A. x arendsii** is a group of hybrids with many available cultivars, including **'Avalanche'** with white flowers, **'Cattleya'** with pale pink flowers, and **'Fanal'** with red flowers. **A. chinensis** var. **pumila** is a dense, vigorous, low-growing, spreading perennial that tolerates dry soil better than other astilbe species. **A. japonica** is a compact, clump-forming perennial. The species is rarely grown in favor of the many cultivars, including **'Deutschland'** with white flowers and **'Peach Blossom'** with peachy pink flowers.

Features: attractive foliage; white, pink, purple, peach, red summer flowers
Height: 10–48" **Spread:** 8–36"
Hardiness: zones 3–9

Black-Eyed Susan
Rudbeckia

Black-eyed Susan is a tough, low-maintenance, long-lived perennial. Plant it wherever you want a casual look. Black-eyed Susan looks great planted in drifts.

Growing

Black-eyed Susans grow well in **full sun** or **partial shade**. The soil should be of **average fertility** and **well drained**. Several *Rudbeckia* species are touted as 'claybusters' for their tolerance of fairly heavy clay soils. Established plants are drought tolerant but regular watering is best. Divide in spring or fall, every three to five years.

Tips

Include these native plants in wildflower and natural gardens, beds and borders. Pinching the plants in June will result in shorter, bushier stands.

Recommended

R. fulgida is an upright, spreading plant bearing orange-yellow flowers with brown centers. **Var. sullivantii** **'Goldsturm'** bears large, bright golden yellow flowers.

R. 'Herbstsonne' is an upright, clump-forming perennial that produces bright yellow, daisy-like flowers with prominent green centers that face up to the sky. The flowers are produced from mid-summer to early autumn.

R. laciniata (cutleaf coneflower) forms a large, open clump. The yellow flowers have green centers. **'Goldquelle'** has bright yellow, double flowers.

R. fulgida with coneflowers (above)
R. 'Herbstsonne' (below)

The flowers last well when cut for arrangements.

Features: bright yellow, orange, red flowers, with centers typically brown or green; attractive foliage; easy to grow **Height:** 24–72" **Spread:** 18–36" **Hardiness:** zones 3–8

Cardinal Flower
Lobelia

L. cardinalis (above & below)

The brilliant red of these flowers is motivation enough for some gardeners to install a pond or bog garden,

These lovely members of the bellflower family contain deadly alkaloids and have poisoned people who tried to use them in herbal medicines.

just to meet cardinal flowers' moist soil requirements.

Growing
Cardinal flowers grow well in **full sun, light shade** or **partial shade**. The soil should be **fertile, slightly acidic** and **moist**. Avoid letting the soil dry out completely, especially in a sunny location. Mulch plants lightly in winter for protection. Deadhead to keep the plants neat and to encourage a possible second flush of blooms. Plants tend to self-seed, but seedlings may not be identical to parent plants. Seedlings can be moved to new locations or they can be left where they are to replace the short-lived parent plants when they die.

Tips
These plants are best suited to streamside or pondside plantings or in bog gardens. They can also be included in moist beds and borders or in any location where they will be watered regularly.

Recommended
L. cardinalis forms an upright clump of bronze-green leaves and bears spikes of bright red flowers from summer to fall. There are also many hybrids and cultivars available, often with flowers in shades of blue, purple, red or pink. Some hybrids and cultivars are as hardy as the species while others are not as hardy.

Features: bright red, purple, blue, pink summer flowers; bronze-green foliage
Height: 24–48" **Spread:** 12–24"
Hardiness: zones 4–9

Catmint
Nepeta

N. x *faassenii* 'Walker's Low' (above), *N.* x *faassenii* (below)

The real workhorses of the garden bed, catmints offer season-long blooms on sturdy, trouble-free plants.

Growing
These plants prefer **full sun** in coastal areas and **partial shade** inland. Grow them in **well-drained** soil of **average fertility**; the growth tends to flop in rich soil. Plant in spring; divide in spring or fall when they look overgrown and dense.

In June, pinch the tips to delay flowering and make the plants more compact.

Tips
Catmints form upright, spreading clumps. Plant them in herb gardens, perennial beds, rock gardens, cottage gardens with roses or for edging borders and pathways.

Take care if you decide to grow *N. cataria* (catnip) because cats are extremely attracted to this plant. Cats do like the other species, but not as much.

Recommended
N. x *faassenii* bears blue or purple flowers. Cultivars with gray-green foliage and pink, white, light purple or lavender blue flowers are available, as are low-growing cultivars.

N. **'Six Hills Giant'** bears deep lavender blue flowers.

Like all members of the mint family, catnip has square stems.

Features: aromatic foliage; attractive blue, purple, white, pink flowers; easy to grow
Height: 18–36" **Spread:** 12–24"
Hardiness: zones 3–8

Chrysanthemum

Chrysanthemum

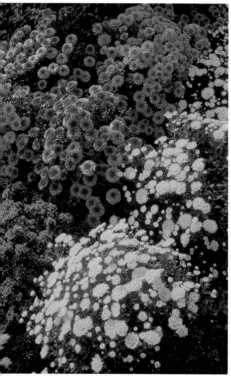

C. hybrids (above & below)

Although the name Chrysanthemum *comes from the Greek and means 'golden flower,' these plants actually bloom in a wide range of bright colors.*

Perk up your fall garden with a bright display of fall 'mums' and their masses of colorful flowers.

Growing

Chrysanthemums grow best in **full sun**. The soil should be **fertile, moist** and **well drained**. Plant as early in the growing season as possible to increase the chances that chrysanthemums will survive winter. Pinch plants back in early summer to encourage bushy growth and to increase flower production. Divide plants every two or three years to keep them growing well.

Tips

Chrysanthemums provide a blaze of color in the fall garden that lasts until the first hard frost. In groups, or as specimen plants, they can be included in borders, in planters or in plantings by the house. If they are purchased in fall, they can be added to spots where summer annuals have faded.

Recommended

C. hybrids form a diverse group of plant series. A few popular hybrids are **C. 'Mei-Kyo,'** a vigorous grower that produces deep pink flowers in mid- to late October, and the **C. 'Prophet' Series** that has cultivars with flowers in a wide range of colors, including **'Christine'** with deep, salmon pink flowers and **'Raquel'** with bright red flowers.

Features: late-summer or fall flowers in every color and combination except blue
Height: 12–36" **Spread:** 24–48"
Hardiness: zones 5–9

Columbine

Aquilegia

*D*elicate and beautiful columbines add a touch of simple elegance to any garden. Blooming from spring through to mid-summer, these long-lasting flowers herald the passing of cool spring weather and the arrival of summer.

Growing

Columbines grow well in **light shade** or **partial shade**. They prefer soil that is **fertile, moist** and **well drained** but adapt to most soil conditions. Division is not required but can be done to propagate desirable plants. Divided plants may take a while to recover because columbines dislike having their roots disturbed.

Tips

Use columbines in rock gardens, formal or casual borders and naturalized or woodland gardens. Place them where other plants can fill in to hide the foliage as the columbines die back over summer.

If leaf miners are a problem, cut the foliage back once flowering is complete and new foliage will fill in.

Recommended

A. alpina (alpine columbine) grows 1–2' tall and 1' wide, bearing nodding, bright blue flowers.

A. canadensis (wild columbine, Canada columbine) is a native plant that is common in woodlands and fields. It bears yellow flowers with red spurs.

A. canadensis (above)
A. x hybrida 'McKana Giants' (below)

A. chrysantha (golden columbine) is a large, many branched species with upright, bright yellow flowers with hooked spurs. This species can grow 3–4' tall.

A. x hybrida (*A. x cultorum*; hybrid columbine) forms mounds of delicate foliage and has exceptional flowers. Many hybrids have been developed with showy flowers in a wide range of colors.

A. vulgaris (European columbine, common columbine) has been used to develop many hybrids and cultivars with flowers in a variety of colors and forms, including double-flowered cultivars that look like frilly dahlias.

Features: spring and summer flowers in shades of red, yellow, pink, purple, blue, white; color of spurs often differs from that of the petals; attractive foliage **Height:** 18–48" **Spread:** 12–24" **Hardiness:** zones 3–8

Coneflower

Echinacea

E. purpurea (above & below)

Coneflower is a visual delight with its mauve petals offset by a spiky, orange center.

Growing

Coneflower grows well in **full sun** or very **light shade**. It tolerates any well-drained soil but prefers an **average to rich** soil. The thick taproots make this plant drought resistant, but it prefers to have regular water. Divide every four or five years in spring or autumn.

Deadhead early in the season to prolong flowering. Later you may wish to leave the flowerheads in place to self-seed to provide winter interest. Pinch plants back or thin out the stems in early summer to promote bushy growth that will be less prone to mildew.

Tips

Use coneflowers in meadow gardens and informal borders, either in groups or as single specimens.

The dry flowerheads make an interesting feature in autumn and winter gardens.

Recommended

E. **'Paranoia'** is the result of crossing *E. paradoxa* and *E. purpurea*. It grows 1' wide and tall, bearing rigid, yellow flowers with prominent, fuzzy, brown centers that point up to the sky.

E. purpurea is an upright plant that is covered in prickly hairs. It bears purple flowers with orangy centers. Cultivars are available, including selections with white or pink flowers. Some new hybrids offer an expanded color range of orange or yellow flowers.

Features: mid-summer to autumn purple, pink, yellow, orange, white flowers with rusty orange or brown centers; persistent seedheads
Height: 24–60" **Spread:** 12–24"
Hardiness: zones 3–8

Coral Bells
Heuchera

From soft yellow-greens and oranges to midnight purples and silvery, dappled maroons, coral bells offer a great variety of foliage options for a perennial garden with partial shade.

Growing

Coral bells grow best in **light** or **partial shade**. The foliage colors can bleach out in full sun, and plants grow leggy in full shade. The soil should be of **average to rich fertility, humus rich, neutral to alkaline, moist** and **well drained**. Good air circulation is essential. Deadhead to prolong blooming.

Every two or three years, coral bells should be dug up and the oldest, woodiest roots and stems removed. Plants may be divided at this time, if desired, then replanted with the crown at or just above soil level.

Tips

Use coral bells as edging plants, in clusters and woodland gardens, or as groundcover in low-traffic areas. Combine different foliage types for an interesting display.

Recommended

There are dozens of beautiful cultivars available with almost limitless variations of foliage markings and colors. See your local garden center or a mail-order catalog to discover what is available.

H. x brizioides 'Firefly' (above), *H. sanguineum* (below)

Coral bells have a strange habit of pushing themselves up out of the soil because of their shallow root systems. Mulch in autumn if the plants begin heaving from the ground.

Features: very decorative foliage; red, pink, white, yellow, purple spring or summer flowers
Height: 12–48" **Spread:** 6–18"
Hardiness: zones 3–9

Daylily
Hemerocallis

The daylily's adaptability and durability combined with its variety in color, blooming period, size and texture explain this perennial's popularity.

Growing
Daylilies grow in any light from **full sun to full shade**. The deeper the shade, the fewer flowers will be produced. The soil should be **fertile, moist** and **well drained,** but these plants adapt to most conditions and are hard to kill once established.

Divide every two or three years to keep plants vigorous and to propagate them. They can, however, be left indefinitely without dividing. Deadhead to prolong the blooming period.

Be careful when deadheading purple-flowered daylilies because the sap can stain fingers and clothes.

Tips
Plant daylilies alone, or group them in borders, on banks and in ditches to control erosion. They can be naturalized in woodland or meadow gardens. Small varieties are also nice in planters.

Recommended
Daylilies come in an almost infinite number of forms, sizes and colors in a range of species, cultivars and hybrids. Visit your local garden center or daylily grower to find out what's available and most suitable for your garden.

'Dewey Roquemore' (above), 'Bonanza' (below)

Features: spring and summer flowers in every color except blue and pure white; grass-like foliage **Height:** 12–48" **Spread:** 12–48" **Hardiness:** zones 2–8

Gayfeather
Liatris

Gayfeather is an outstanding cut flower with fuzzy, spiked blossoms above grass-like foliage. It is also an excellent plant for attracting butterflies to the garden.

Growing

Gayfeather prefers **full sun**. The soil should be of **average fertility, sandy** and **humus rich**. Water well during the growing season but don't allow the plants to stand in water during cool weather. Mulch during summer to prevent moisture loss.

Trim off the spent flower spikes to promote a longer blooming period and to keep gayfeather looking tidy. Divide every three or four years in autumn. The clump will appear crowded when it is time to divide.

Tips

Use gayfeather in borders and meadow plantings. Plant it in a location that has good drainage to avoid root rot in winter. Gayfeather also grows well in planters.

Recommended

L. spicata is a clump-forming, erect plant. The flowers are pinkish purple or white. Several cultivars are available, including **'Floristan White,'** bearing tall, white flower spikes, and **'Kobold'** that bears deep purple blooms.

L. spicata 'Kobold' (above), *L. spicata* (below)

The spikes make excellent, long-lasting cut flowers.

Also called: spike gayfeather
Features: purple or white summer flowers; grass-like foliage **Height:** 18–36"
Spread: 18–24" **Hardiness:** zones 3–9

Heliopsis
Heliopsis

H. helianthoides (above & below)

The stems of heliopsis are stiff, making the blooms useful in fresh arrangements.

*O*f flowers send messages, heliopsis sings out, 'It's fun in the sun!' Combine these bright characters with butterfly weed, asters and ornamental grasses for a look that is unforgettable.

Growing

Heliopsis prefers **full sun** but tolerates partial shade. The soil should be **average to fertile, humus rich, moist** and **well drained**. Most soil conditions are tolerated, including poor, dry soils. Divide every two or three years.

Deadhead to prolong the blooming period. Cut plants back once flowering is complete.

Tips

Use heliopsis at the back or in the middle of mixed or herbaceous borders. This plant is easy to grow and popular with novice gardeners.

Recommended

H. helianthoides forms an upright clump of stems and foliage and bears yellow or orange, daisy-like flowers. A variety of cultivars are available offering unique characteristics, including **'Summer Sun'** ('Sommersonne') that bears single or semi-double flowers in bright golden yellow. It grows about 36" tall.

Features: bright yellow or orange flowers
Height: 3–5' **Spread:** 18–36"
Hardiness: zones 2–9

Hosta

Hosta

Breeders are always looking for new variations in hosta foliage. Swirls, stripes, puckers and ribs enhance the leaves' various sizes, shapes and colors.

Growing

Hostas prefer **light** or **partial shade** but will grow in full shade. Morning sun is preferable to afternoon sun in partial shade situations. The soil should be **fertile, moist** and **well drained** but most soils are tolerated. Hostas are fairly drought tolerant, especially if given a mulch to help them retain moisture.

Division is not required but can be done every few years in spring or summer to propagate new plants.

Tips

Hostas make wonderful woodland plants and look very attractive when combined with ferns and other fine-textured plants. Hostas are also good plants for a mixed border, particularly when used to hide the ugly, leggy, lower stems and branches of some shrubs. Hostas' dense growth and thick, shade-providing leaves allow them to suppress weeds.

Recommended

Hostas have been subjected to a great deal of crossbreeding and hybridizing, resulting in hundreds of cultivars. Visit your local garden center or get a mail-order catalog to find out what's available.

H. fortunei 'Francee' (above)

Some gardeners think the flowers clash with the foliage, and they remove the flower stems when they first emerge. If you find the flowers unattractive, removing them won't harm the plant.

Also called: plantain lily Features: decorative foliage; summer and autumn flowers in white or purple Height: 4–36"
Spread: 6–72" Hardiness: zones 3–8

Japanese Anemone
Anemone

A. x *hybrida* (above & below)

Growing

Japanese anemone prefers **partial or light shade** but tolerates full sun. The soil should be of **average to high fertility, humus rich** and **moist**. Allow the soil to dry out when plants are dormant. Mulch the first winter to allow plants to become established. Deadheading will keep plants tidy but will not prolong the blooming period.

Tips

Japanese anemones make a beautiful addition to lightly shaded borders, woodland gardens and cottage gardens.

Recommended

A. *huphensis* (Chinese anemone) is an erect perennial with long stalks, dark green ornate foliage and white or pink, single flowers. This species will grow 24–36" tall and 16" wide. Other selections are available in a wide variety of colors, including **var. *japonica* 'Party Dress,'** bearing double, pink flowers with bright yellow centers, and **'September Charm,'** bearing pale pink blossoms.

A. x *hybrida* is an upright plant with a suckering habit. Flowers in shades of pink or white are produced in late summer and early fall. Many cultivars are available, including **'Honorine Jobert,'** bearing white flowers with a touch of pink on the reverse, and **'Pamina,'** a semi-double, lavender pink selection.

As the rest of the garden begins to fade in late summer, Japanese anemone is just beginning its fall show. The white and pink colors are a welcome sight in the fall garden that is usually dominated by yellow and orange.

The name 'windflower' was given to describe the plumy seeds that are carried away on the wind.

Also called: windflower **Features:** pink or white late-summer to fall flowers; attractive foliage **Height:** 2–5' **Spread:** 2' **Hardiness:** zones 5–9

Lamb's Ears

Stachys

S. byzantina 'Helene von Stein' (above), *S. byzantina* (below)

L amb's ears' soft, fuzzy leaves give this perennial its common names. The silvery foliage is a beautiful contrast to bold-colored plants that tower above; it softens hard lines and surfaces.

Growing

Lamb's ears grows best in **full sun.** The soil should be of **poor** or **average fertility** and **well drained.** The leaves can rot in humid weather if the soil is poorly drained. Remove spent flower spikes to keep plants looking neat.

Tips

Lamb's ears makes a great groundcover in a new garden where the soil has not yet been amended. It can be used to edge borders and pathways because it provides a soft, silvery backdrop for more vibrant colors in the border.

Recommended

S. byzantina forms a mat of thick, woolly rosettes of leaves. Pinkish purple flowers bloom all summer. There are many cultivars that offer a variety of foliage colors, sizes and flowers, including **'Helene von Stein'** that produces fuzzy leaves twice as large as other species or cultivars. **'Primrose Heron'** produces yellowish gray leaves.

Like many plants in the mint family, lamb's ears contains antibacterial and antifungal compounds. It not only feels soft, but may actually encourage healing.

Also called: lamb's tails, lamb's tongues
Features: soft and fuzzy, silver or gray foliage; pink or purple flowers **Height:** 6–18"
Spread: 18–24" **Hardiness:** zones 3–8

Lenten Rose

Helleborus

H. foetidus (above & below)

These beautiful, spring-blooming groundcover plants are among the earliest harbingers of spring, providing the welcome sight of what's to come long before most other plants have even started to sprout.

Growing

Lenten rose prefers **light, dappled shade** and a **sheltered location** but tolerates some direct sun if the soil stays evenly moist. The soil should be **fertile, humus rich, neutral to alkaline, moist** and **well drained**. Mulch plants in winter if they are in an exposed location. In a mild winter the leaves may stay evergreen, and flowers may appear as early as February.

Tips

Use these plants in a sheltered border or rock garden, or naturalize in a woodland garden.

Recommended

H. foetidus (bear's-foot hellebore) grows 2' tall and wide. It bears dark green leaves and clusters of light green flowers with purplish red edges. Larger cultivars are available with varied flower colors.

H. x hybridus plants grow about 18" tall, with an equal spread. Plants may be deciduous or evergreen, and they bloom in a wide range of colors. Some cultivars have deeper-colored flowers, double flowers, spotted flowers or picotee flowers.

H. orientalis (lenten rose) is a clump-forming, evergreen perennial. It grows 12–24" tall, with an equal spread. It bears white or greenish flowers that turn pink as they mature in mid- or late spring.

Features: late-winter to mid-spring flowers in white, green, pink, purple, yellow
Height: 12–24" **Spread:** 12–24"
Hardiness: zones 5–9

Lily Turf
Liriope

Often confused with mondo grass or *Ophiopogon*, this grass-like perennial is commonly used throughout the South because of its showy flowers, clump-forming growth habit and use as a groundcover and border edging.

Growing

Lily turf prefers locations with **full to partial sun. Light, moderately fertile** soil that is **moist, slightly acidic** and **well drained** is best.

Tips

Lily turf is often planted in rows along border edges to create a defined, ornate line that separates the bed from pathways, sidewalks, patios and driveways.

Recommended

L. muscari is a clump-forming perennial with arching, grass-like foliage. Flower spikes emerge from the crown that support bright purple flowers in late summer. Cultivars are available with white flowers, and golden variegated, solid and silvery foliage. **'Big Blue'** bears violet blue flowers, and **'Monroe White'** produces white flower spikes held above dark green foliage. **'Variegata'** produces green leaves with creamy yellow edges and purple flowers.

L. muscari (above), *L. muscari* 'Variegata' (below)

The flowers are followed by small, black berry-like fruit.

Features: purple, violet blue, white flowers; grass-like foliage in dense clumps **Height:** 1–2'
Spread: 1–2' **Hardiness:** zones 6–10

Obedient Plant
Physostegia

P. virginiana 'Variegata' (above), *P. virginiana* (below)

The individual flowers can be bent around on the stems and will stay put where you leave them. It is this unusual habit that gives the plant its common name.

Hummingbirds love to sip from the miniscule, snapdragon-like flowers, so place your obedient plant where you can watch the show.

Growing

Obedient plants prefer **full sun** but tolerate partial or light shade. The soil should be **moist** and of **average to high fertility**. In a fertile soil these plants are more vigorous and may need staking. Plants can become invasive. Divide in early to mid-spring, once the soil can be worked, every two or three years to curtail invasiveness.

Tips

Use these plants in borders, cottage gardens and for naturalizing. The flowers of obedient plants can be cut for use in fresh arrangements.

Recommended

P. virginiana has a spreading root system from which upright stems sprout. The species bears sharply toothed foliage and deep purple or bright purple-pink and, sometimes, white flower spikes. The species can grow to 4' tall, and cultivars are available in smaller, compact forms with pink, white or purple flowers. **'Pink Bouquet'** bears bright pink flowers, and **'Variegata'** produces variegated foliage with creamy margined leaves and bright pink flowers.

Features: mid-summer to fall, purple, pink, white flowers; habit **Height:** 1–4' **Spread:** 1–2' **Hardiness:** zones 2–9

Peony
Paeonia

From the simple, single flowers to the extravagant doubles, it's easy to become mesmerized with these voluptuous plants. Once the fleeting, but magnificent, flower display is done, the foliage remains stellar throughout the growing season.

Growing

Peonies prefer **full sun** but tolerate some shade. The planting site should be well prepared before the plants are introduced. Peonies like **fertile, humus-rich, moist, well-drained** soil to which a lot of compost has been added. Mulch peonies lightly with compost in spring. Too much fertilizer, particularly nitrogen, causes floppy growth and retards blooming. Deadhead to keep plants looking tidy.

Tips

These wonderful plants look great in a border combined with other early bloomers. They can be underplanted with bulbs and other plants that will die down by mid-summer; the emerging foliage of the peonies hides the dying foliage of the spring plants. Avoid planting peonies under trees, where they will have to compete for moisture and nutrients.

Planting depth determines whether a peony will flower. Tubers planted too shallow or, more commonly, too deep, will not flower. The buds or eyes on the tuber should be 1–2" below the soil surface.

P. *lactiflora* 'Shimmering Velvet' (above)
P. *lactiflora* cultivars (below)

Recommended

There are hundreds of peonies available. Cultivars come in a wide range of colors, may have single or double flowers, and may or may not be fragrant. Visit your local garden center to see what is available.

Place wire peony rings or grids around the plants in early spring to support the heavy flowers. The foliage will grow up and through the wires and hide the ring.

Features: white, cream, yellow, pink, red, purple spring and early-summer flowers; attractive foliage **Height:** 24–32"
Spread: 24–32" **Hardiness:** zones 2–8

Phlox

Phlox

P. subulata (above), *P. paniculata* cultivar (below)

Phlox comes in many shapes and sizes with flowering periods falling anywhere between early spring and mid-autumn.

Growing

Phlox prefers **full sun** and **fertile, humus-rich, moist, well-drained** soil. Divide in autumn or spring.

Tips

Low-growing species are useful in rock gardens or at the front of borders. Taller phloxes may be used in the middle of borders and are particularly effective if planted in groups.

Recommended

P. maculata (Carolina phlox, thick-leaf phlox, early phlox, garden phlox,

wild sweet William) forms an upright clump of hairy stems and narrow leaves that are sometimes spotted with red. Pink, purple or white flowers are borne in conical clusters.

P. paniculata (garden phlox, summer phlox) is an upright plant. The many cultivars vary in size and flower color, including **'Becky Towe,'** which bears salmon-colored flowers with a dark eye and golden variegated foliage.

P. stolonifera (creeping phlox) is a low, spreading plant that bears flowers in several shades of purple. **'Sherwood Purple'** bears deep lavender flowers.

P. subulata (moss phlox, moss pink) is very low growing and produces flowers in various colors. The foliage is evergreen.

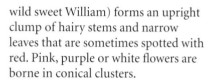

Features: spring, summer or autumn flowers in shades of white, blue, purple, pink, red, salmon, bicolored, often with a colored or contrasting central eye **Height:** 3–5' **Spread:** 1–2' **Hardiness:** zones 4–8

Red-Hot Poker

Kniphofia

his perennial is a great companion plant to many ornamental grasses and requires little to produce the fiery, spiky blooms.

Growing

These plants grow equally well in **full sun** or **partial shade**. The soil should be **fertile, humus rich, sandy** and **moist**. Ensure red-hot pokers receive adequate water when they are blooming. Large clumps may be divided in late spring, or in summer if the plant is flowering in spring. The plants perform best when left undivided for several years.

Tips

Red-hot pokers make a bold, vertical statement in the middle or back of a border. They look best when planted in groups made up of odd numbers. To encourage the plants to continue flowering for as long as possible, cut off the spent flowers where the flower stem emerges from the crown.

Recommended

K. hybrids include a vast number of selections but generally share the same narrow leaves and blooming period of *K. uvaria*. The fiery colors range from dusty coral and creamy white to tangerine orange and glowing yellow. **'Flamenco'** produces flowers in shades of coral, orange, apricot or cream. **'Little Maid'** has creamy yellow flowers.

K. hybrids (above & below)

K. uvaria produces spikes of drooping, bright red to orange-red flower buds that open to yellow from late summer to early fall. Many cultivars are available in varied mature sizes and flower colors.

The flowers of red-hot poker are attractive to hummingbirds and butterflies. The blooms make long-lasting cut flowers and add bold accents to any floral arrangement.

Features: orange, yellow, apricot, cream, chartreuse, red, white, coral flower spikes; overall form **Height:** 3–4'
Spread: 18–24" **Hardiness:** zones 5–9

Russian Sage
Perovskia

P. atriplicifolia 'Longin' with coneflowers (above)
P. atriplicifolia Cultivar (below)

Russian sage blossoms make a lovely addition to fresh bouquets and dried-flower arrangements.

Russian sage offers four-season interest in the garden: soft, gray-green leaves on light gray stems in spring; fuzzy, violet blue flowers in summer; and silvery white stems in autumn that last until late winter.

Growing
Russian sage prefers **full sun**. The soil should be **poor to moderately fertile** and **well drained**. Too much water and nitrogen will cause this plant's growth to flop, so do not plant it next to heavy feeders. Russian sage cannot be divided because it is a subshrub that originates from a single stem.

In spring, when new growth appears low on the branches, or in autumn, cut the plant back hard to about 6–12" to encourage vigorous, bushy growth.

Tips
The silvery foliage and blue flowers soften the appearance of daylilies and work well with other plants in the back of a mixed border. Russian sage can also create a soft screen in a natural garden or on a dry bank.

Recommended
P. atriplicifolia is a loose, upright plant with silvery white, finely divided foliage. The small, lavender blue flowers are loosely held on silvery, branched stems. Cultivars are available, including **'Longin,'** an erect, upright selection with violet blue flowers, and **'Little Spire,'** which is a smaller selection.

Features: blue, purple mid-summer to autumn flowers; attractive habit; fragrant, gray-green foliage **Height:** 3–4'
Spread: 3–4' **Hardiness:** zones 4–9

Sedum

Sedum

Sedum is a large and diverse genus of over 300 different species, including many that do very well in the South.

Growing

Sedums prefer **full sun** but tolerate partial shade. The soil should be of **average fertility** and **very well drained**. Divide these plants in spring when needed.

Tips

Low-growing sedum selections make wonderful groundcovers and additions to rock gardens, rock walls, beds and borders. Taller sedums are excellent for a late-season display in a bed or border.

Recommended

Low-growing, wide-spreading selections (2–6" tall and 24" wide) include **S. acre** (golden teardrop), an aggressive species that bears small, yellow-green flowers; **S. reflexum** (stone orpine) that has blue-green, needle-like foliage (zones 6–9); and **S. spurium** (two-row stonecrop), which has deep pink or white flowers. Many cultivars with colorful foliage are available. Tall selections (18–24" tall and wide) include **S. 'Neon'** that bears intense, deep purplish pink flowers, and **S. spectabile** (showy stonecrop), which blooms in white and in various shades of pink.

S. *spurium* 'Dragon's Blood' (above)
S. 'Autumn Joy' (below)

Early-summer pruning of upright species and hybrids encourages compact, bushy growth but can delay flowering

Also called: stonecrop **Features:** yellow, yellow-green, white, red, pink summer to autumn flowers; decorative, fleshy foliage **Height:** 2–24" **Spread:** 10–24" or more **Hardiness:** zones 3–8

Shasta Daisy
Leucanthemum

L. x superbum cultivars (above & below)

Shasta daisy is one of the most popular perennials because it is easy to grow and the blooms are bright, plentiful and work well as cut flowers.

Growing
Shasta daisy grows well in **full sun** or **partial shade**. The soil should be **fertile, moist** and **well drained**. Pinch or trim plants back in spring to encourage compact, bushy growth. Divide every year or two, in spring, to maintain plant vigor. Fall-planted Shasta daisy may not become established in time to

Three years is a good lifespan for most Shasta daisy plants in Virginia because our heavy soil rarely drains well enough to ensure winter hardiness.

survive winter. Plants can be short-lived in zones 4 and 5.

Deadheading extends the bloom by several weeks. Start seeds indoors in spring or direct sow into warm soil.

Tips
Use Shasta daisy as a single plant or massed in groups. Shorter varieties can be used in many garden settings, and taller varieties may need support if exposed to windy situations. The flowers can be cut for fresh arrangements.

Recommended
L. x **superbum** forms a large clump of dark green leaves and stems. It bears white daisy flowers with yellow centers all summer, often until first frost. **'Becky'** has strong, wind-resistant stems, with blooms lasting up to eight weeks. **'Craisy Daisy'** bears double, 2" wide, white blooms.

Features: white early-summer to fall flowers with yellow centers **Height:** 12"–4' **Spread:** 15–24" **Hardiness:** zones 4–9

Showy Evening Primrose

Oenothera

Showy evening primrose are native plants that do very well in Virginia gardens.

Growing

Showy evening primrose prefers **full sun**. The soil should be of **poor to average fertility** and **very well drained**. These plants can become invasive in fertile soil. They aren't bothered by hot, humid weather. Divide showy evening primrose in spring.

Tips

Use these plants in the front of a border and to edge borders and pathways. They will brighten a gravelly bank or rock garden.

Showy evening primrose self-seeds and finds its way into unexpected places.

Recommended

O. fruticosa (sundrops) grows 12–18" tall and wide. It bears bright yellow flowers in summer. The foliage of this plant turns red after a light frost. **'Fireworks'** has red stems and yellow blooms that open from red buds.

O. speciosa (showy evening primrose) is a lanky, upright or spreading plant. It grows 10–12" tall and wide. Its flowers can be pink or white.

O. speciosa (above), *O. fruticosa* (below)

Another common name for these plants is 'evening star,' because at night the petals emit phosphorescent light.

Also called: sundrops Features: yellow, pink, white summer flowers; easy to grow
Height: 10–18" Spread: 10–18"
Hardiness: zones 3–8

Spiked Speedwell
Veronica

V. 'Sunny Border Blue' (above)
V. spicata 'Red Fox' (below)

Spiked speedwell combines well with lilies, yarrow, shrub roses and daisy-flowered perennials.

Spiked speedwell punctuates the front or middle of a garden bed with spikes of white, pink or violet flowers.

Growing
Spiked speedwell prefers **full sun** but tolerates partial shade. The soil should be of **average fertility, moist** and **well drained**. Once established, this perennial will tolerate short periods of drought. Lack of sun and excessive moisture and nitrogen may be partly to blame for the sloppy habits of some speedwells. Divide every two or three years in spring to ensure strong, vigorous growth and to reduce flopping.

When the flowers begin to fade, remove the entire spike where it joins the plant to encourage rapid re-blooming.

Tips
Spiked speedwell works well at the front of a perennial border, as a groundcover or contained in a rock garden. It is also quite striking when planted in masses in a bed or border.

Recommended
V. spicata is a low, mounding plant with stems that flop over when they get too tall. It bears spikes of blue flowers. Many cultivars with different flower colors are available, including **'Royal Candles,'** which bears blue-purple flowers for an exceptionally long period of time.

Features: white, pink, purple, blue summer flowers; varied habits **Height:** 6–24"
Spread: 12–24" **Hardiness:** zones 3–8

Tickseed
Coreopsis

These plants produce flowers all summer and are easy to grow; they make a fabulous addition to any garden.

Growing

Tickseed grow best in **full sun**. The soil should be of **average fertility, sandy, light** and **well drained**. Plants can develop crown rot in moist, cool locations with heavy soil. Too fertile a soil will encourage floppy growth. Deadhead to keep plants blooming.

Tips

Tickseed are versatile plants, useful in formal and informal borders and in meadow plantings and cottage gardens. They look best when planted in groups.

Recommended

C. auriculata 'Nana' (mouse-eared tickseed) is a low-growing species, well suited to rock gardens and the fronts of borders. It grows about 12" tall and spreads indefinitely, though slowly. It bears yellow-orange flowers in late spring.

C. grandiflora (bigflower coreopsis) is a clump-forming perennial that is often grown as an annual because of its prolific blooming cycle. It produces bright yellow flowers atop slender stems that grow 1–2' tall. A number of cultivar selections are available with semi-double and double flowers, differing bloom times and varied sizes.

C. rosea (rose coreopsis) is a finely textured perennial with bright green

C. verticillata (above), C. grandiflora (below)

foliage and pink flowers with yellow centers from summer to fall. '**American Dream**' has deep rose pink flowers over fine-textured foliage.

C. verticillata (thread-leaf coreopsis) is a mound-forming plant with attractive, finely divided foliage and bright yellow flowers. It grows 24–32" tall and spreads 18". Available cultivars include selections with pale yellow blooms and smaller, mature sizes.

Features: yellow, orange, white, pink summer flowers; attractive foliage **Height:** 12–32"
Spread: 12" to indefinite
Hardiness: zones 3–9

Verbena

Verbena

V. x hybrida (above), *V. canadensis* (below)

Verbenas offer butterflies a banquet. Butterfly visitors include tiger swallowtails, silver-spotted skippers, great spangled fritillaries and painted ladies.

Growing

Verbenas grow best in **full sun**. The soil should be of average **fertility** and **very well drained**. Verbena is drought tolerant when established. Cut or pinch plants back by one-half in mid-summer to encourage a lot of fall blooms.

Tips

Use verbenas in the front or middle of beds and borders, and to add height to containers. Verbena self-seeds in abundance, but the seedlings are easy to keep under control. Because it is such a wispy plant in flower, verbena looks best when mass planted.

Recommended

V. canadensis (rose verbena) is a perennial that's often grown as an annual. It bears rosy purple flowers atop a compact form. The species grows 18" tall and 18–36" wide. Cultivars are available in smaller forms, including '**Homestead Red**,' a vigorous, spreading plant with mildew-resistant foliage, and '**Homestead Purple**,' bearing dark purple flowers with glossy foliage.

V. x hybrida (garden verbena) is a short-lived perennial that is often grown as an annual. This hybrid is densely branched, producing grayish green foliage and compact clusters of white, pink, bright red, purple or blue flowers, both in solid colors and sometimes in combinations. Other selections are available in colorful variations. '**Taylortown Red**' is a fine example of a red-blooming garden verbena.

Features: purple, blue, red, white, pink, peach flowers in early to late summer; growth habit
Height: 6–18" **Spread:** 18–36"
Hardiness: zones 6–9

Arborvitae

Thuja

*A*rborvitae are rot resistant, durable and long-lived, earning quiet admiration from gardeners everywhere.

Growing

Arborvitae prefer **partial shade** but tolerate light to partial shade. The soil should be of **average fertility, moist** and **well drained**. These plants enjoy humidity and are often found growing near marshy areas in the wild. Arborvitae perform best in a location sheltered from wind, especially in winter.

Tips

The larger varieties of arborvitae make excellent specimen trees; smaller cultivars can be used in foundation plantings and shrub borders and as formal or informal hedges.

Recommended

T. occidentalis (American arborvitae) is a narrow, pyramidal tree with scale-like, evergreen needles. Dozens of cultivars are available, including shrubby dwarf varieties, varieties with yellow foliage and smaller, upright varieties. (Zones 2–7; some cultivars may be less cold hardy)

T. orientalis (oriental arborvitae) grows 25' tall and 15' wide. The species is rarely available, but the cultivars and hybrids are highly sought after for their varied colorations, forms and overall diversity. Two popular selections are **'Aurea Nana,'** producing golden foliage in a compact, globe form, and **'Blue Cone,'** which is a dense, upright form with bluish green coloration.

T. occidentalis 'Yellow Ribbon' (above)
T. occidentalis (below)

T. plicata (western arborvitae, western red cedar) is a narrowly pyramidal evergreen tree that grows quickly, resists deer browsing and maintains good foliage color all winter. Several cultivars are available, including several dwarf varieties and a yellow and green variegated variety. **'Green Giant'** can grow 3–5' annually, eventually growing 30–50' tall with a spread of 10–20'. (Zones 5–9)

Features: small to large, evergreen shrub or tree; attractive foliage; bark; habit
Height: 2–50' **Spread:** 2–20'
Hardiness: zones 2–8

Azalea • Rhododendron

Rhododendron

Azalea hybrids (above & below)

Even without their flowers, azaleas and rhododendrons are wonderful landscape plants. Their striking, dark green foliage lends an interesting texture to a shrub planting in summer.

Growing

Azaleas prefer **partial shade** or **light shade**, but they tolerate full sun in a site with adequate moisture. A location sheltered from strong winds is preferable. The soil should be **fertile, humus rich, acidic, moist** and very **well drained.** Rhododendrons are sensitive to high pH, salinity and winter injury.

Weevils often make notches along the leaf margins of rhododendrons. The variety 'PJM' is resistant to these insects.

Tips

Use azaleas and rhododendrons in shrub or mixed borders, in woodland gardens, as specimen plants, in group plantings, as hedges and informal barriers, in rock gardens or in planters on a shady patio or balcony.

Azaleas and rhododendrons are generally grouped together. Extensive breeding and hybridizing is making it more and more difficult to label them separately.

Recommended

In our area, we can grow many azalea and rhododendron species and cultivars. In fact, it's even difficult to know where to begin. Many wonderful nurseries and specialty growers can help you find the right azalea or rhododendron for your garden based on your wants and needs.

Features: upright, mounding, rounded, evergreen or deciduous shrub; late-winter to early-summer flowers in almost every color imaginable; foliage **Height:** 2–12' **Spread:** 2–12' **Hardiness:** zones 3–8

Bald-Cypress
Taxodium

Bald-cypress is a tough, dependable tree that can grow well in a variety of conditions and climates.

Growing

Bald-cypress grows well in **full sun** in **moist, acidic** soil, but adapts to most soils and conditions. Highly alkaline soil can cause the foliage to turn yellow. Bald-cypress develops a deep taproot but transplants fairly easily when young.

Tips

Bald-cypress can be used as a specimen tree or in a group planting. This is a fairly large tree that looks best with plenty of space. It is ideal in a swampy or frequently wet area where few other trees would thrive.

When grown in waterlogged soil or near a water feature, bald-cypress develops gnome-like 'knees,' which are knobby roots that poke up from the water.

Recommended

*T. **distichum*** is a slender, conical tree that becomes irregular and more rounded as it matures. In the wild it may grow over 100' tall. In autumn the blue-green foliage turns a rusty orange before falling. The trunk becomes buttressed with age.

T. distichum (above & below)

To the uninformed, bald-cypress appears to be an evergreen. Gasps are often heard when this deciduous conifer turns color in fall and defoliates.

Features: conical, deciduous, coniferous tree; summer and fall foliage; cones; trunk **Height:** 50–100' or more **Spread:** 18–30' **Hardiness:** zones 4–9

Barberry

Berberis

B. thunbergii 'Aurea' (above), *B. thunbergii* 'Atropurpurea' (below)

Barberries are dependable, easy-growing shrubs with many variations in plant size, foliage color and fruit. Barberries are real workhorses in the garden.

Growing

Barberries develop the best fall color and most fruit when grown in **full sun**, but they tolerate partial shade. Any **well-drained** soil is suitable. Barberries tolerate drought and urban conditions but suffer in poorly drained, wet soil.

Tips

Large barberries make great hedges. Barberries can also be included in shrub and mixed borders. Small cultivars can be grown in rock gardens, in raised beds and along rock walls.

Recommended

B. julianae (Wintergreen barberry) is a dense, evergreen shrub with an upright growth habit. It produces small, glossy foliage with lighter undersides and yellow- or red-tinged flowers. This species is one of the spiniest selections available and is often used as hedging material. The flowers are followed by small, black fruit. It grows 6' tall with an equal spread.

B. thunbergii (Japanese barberry) is a broad, rounded, dense shrub with bright green foliage, orange, red or purple fall color, yellow spring flowers and glossy red fruit. Many cultivars have varied foliage color, including shades of purple, yellow and variegated varieties.

Features: prickly deciduous shrub; foliage; yellow- or red-tinged flowers; fruit; formidable spines **Height:** 1–6' **Spread:** 18"–6' **Hardiness:** zones 4–8

Beech

Fagus

F. sylvatica 'Pendula' (above), *F. sylvatica* (below)

The aristocrats of the large shade trees, the majestic beeches are certainly not the fastest growing trees, but they are among the most beautiful.

Growing

Beeches grow equally well in **full sun** or **partial shade**. The soil should be of **average fertility, loamy** and **well drained**, though almost all well-drained soils are tolerated.

American beech doesn't like having its roots disturbed and should be transplanted only when very young. European beech transplants easily and is more tolerant of varied soil conditions than American beech.

Tips

Beeches make excellent specimens. They are also used as shade trees and in woodland gardens. These trees need a lot of space, but the European beech's adaptability to pruning makes it a reasonable choice in a small garden.

Recommended

F. grandifolia (American beech) is a broad-canopied tree, native to most of eastern North America.

F. sylvatica (European beech) is a spectacular, broad tree with a number of interesting cultivars. Several are small enough to use in the home garden, from narrow columnar and weeping varieties to varieties with purple or yellow leaves, or pink, white and green variegated foliage.

Beech nuts are edible when roasted.

Features: large, oval, deciduous shade tree; attractive foliage; bark; fall color; fruit
Height: 30–80' **Spread:** 10–65'
Hardiness: zones 4–8

Black Gum
Nyssa

N. sylvatica (above & below)

Black gum shines with bright green foliage in summer, giving way to a lovely autumn show in shades of yellow, orange, scarlet or purple.

Growing
Black gum grows well in **full sun** or **partial shade**. The soil should be **average to fertile, neutral to acidic** and **well drained**. Provide a location with shelter from strong winds. Plant these trees when they are young, and don't attempt to move them again. They dislike having their roots disturbed and can take awhile to get established after they are planted.

Tips
Black gum is a beautiful specimen tree. It can be used as a street tree but not in polluted situations. Singly or in groups, it is attractive and small enough for a medium-sized property.

Recommended
N. sylvatica is a small- to medium-sized, pyramidal to rounded tree. It generally grows 30–50' tall but can reach 100' over time. It spreads to about 20–30'. Cultivars are available with unique characteristics, including **'Forum,'** which has a conical form.

The fruit attracts birds but is too sour for human tastes.

Features: pyramidal to rounded deciduous tree; summer and fall foliage **Height:** 10–50' or more **Spread:** 6–30' **Hardiness:** zones 4–9

Boxwood

Buxus

Boxwood's dense growth and small leaves form an even, green surface, which, along with its slow rate of growth, make it among the most popular plants for creating low hedges and topiaries.

Growing

Boxwoods prefer **partial shade** but adapt to full sun if kept well watered. The soil should be **fertile** and **well drained**. Once established, these plants are drought tolerant. A good, rich mulch benefits these shrubs because their roots grow very close to the surface. Try not to disturb the soil around established boxwoods because the roots are easily damaged.

Tips

Boxwoods make excellent background plants in a mixed border. Dwarf cultivars can be trimmed into small hedges for edging garden beds or walkways. An interesting topiary piece can create a formal or whimsical focal point in any garden. Larger species and cultivars are often used to form dense, evergreen hedges.

Recommended

B. microphylla **var.** *koreana* grows about 4' tall, with an equal spread. The bright green foliage may turn bronze, brown or yellow in winter. It is hardy to zone 4. Cultivars are available.

B. sempervirens (common boxwood) can grow up to 20' tall, with an equal spread if left unpruned. **'Suffruticosa'** (edging boxwood) is a compact, slow-growing cultivar that's often used as hedging. Other cultivars are also available in varied sizes and forms.

B. sempervirens cultivars (above & below)

Some of the best boxwood selections are cultivars developed from crosses between the two listed species. These hybrids possess a high level of pest resistance, vigor and attractive winter color. **'Green Velvet'** and **'Green Mountain'** are selections well suited for Virginia.

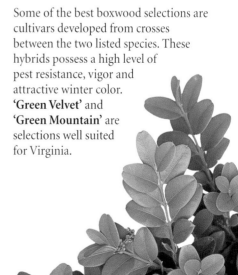

Features: dense, rounded, evergreen shrub; attractive foliage **Height:** 2–20'
Spread: 2–20' **Hardiness:** zones 4–8

Burning Bush

Euonymus

E. alatus 'Cole's Select' (above), *E. alatus* (below)

$\mathcal{F}$ew plants can match the stunning fall color of burning bush, a popular *Euonymus* variety.

Growing
Burning bush species prefer **full sun** but tolerate light or partial shade. Soil of **average to rich fertility** is preferable, but any **moist, well-drained** soil will do.

Tips
Burning bush can be grown in a shrub or mixed border, as a specimen, in a naturalistic garden or as a hedge. Dwarf cultivars can be used to create informal hedges.

Recommended
E. alatus (burning bush, winged euonymus) is an attractive, open, mounding, deciduous shrub with corky ridges on the stems and branches, and vivid red fall foliage. Cultivars are available, including a dwarf selection called **'Compacta.'**

The name Euonymus *means 'of good name,' an ironic translation given that all parts of these plants are **poisonous** and violently purgative.*

Features: deciduous and evergreen shrub, small tree, groundcover or climber; foliage; corky stems **Height:** 2–20' **Spread:** 2–20' **Hardiness:** zones 3–8

Butterfly Bush
Buddleia (Buddleja)

B. davidii (above & below)

Butterfly bushes are among the best shrubs for attracting butterflies and bees to the garden. Don't spray this bush for pests—you will harm the beautiful and beneficial insects that call it home.

Growing
Butterfly bushes prefer to grow in **full sun**. Plants grown in shade will produce few flowers. The soil should be **average to fertile** and **well drained**. These shrubs are drought tolerant once established.

Tips
Its graceful, arching branches make butterfly bush an excellent specimen plant and a beautiful addition to shrub and mixed borders.

To control this very fast-growing shrub, cut it back heavily in the spring, leaving just one-foot stumps. It will bloom that same summer.

Recommended
B. davidii (orange eye butterfly bush, summer lilac) bears flowers in bright and pastel shades of purple, white, pink or blue from mid-summer to fall. Many cultivars are available. (Zones 5–8)

Butterfly bushes can self-seed. You may find tiny bushes popping up in unlikely places around the garden.

Features: deciduous large shrub or small tree with arching branches; flowers in pastel shades of purple, white, pink, blue; foliage
Height: 4–20' **Spread:** 4–20'
Hardiness: zones 4–8

Camellia

Camellia

C. japonica 'Monjisu Red' (above)
C. japonica cultivar (below)

Camellias tolerate salt and pollution, making them excellent choices for coastal and urban plantings.

Growing

Camellias prefer to grow in **light to partial shade** in **well-drained, acidic to neutral** soil that is high in **organic matter**. *C. japonica* prefers more acidic soil.

Protect camellias from strong, hot sun and drying winds. They may also suffer damage if temperatures drop below 15° F.

Tips

Camellias are evergreen plants suitable for mixed beds, borders and woodland gardens, as specimens or as container plants. The soil for container plantings should be 50% organic matter and 50% potting mix.

Recommended

There are almost 300 species of camellias and thousands of cultivars. A few favorites among Virginian gardeners include **C. japonica** (common camellia), which is a large shrub or small tree that varies in growth rate, habit and size. On average, it grows 6–12' tall with an equal spread, but larger specimens do exist in the South. The cultivars are highly sought after for their varied colors, sizes and forms. **C. sasanqua** (sasanqua camellia) produces flowers that are smaller than *C. japonica* but equally beautiful. This species tolerates excessive heat and light and a wider range of soil types, and it produces a more open form. It includes upright, tree-like, shrubby and spreading forms and can grow 6–15' tall. There are many cultivars to choose from in just about every color but blue. **'Dawn'** bears pink flowers; **'Sparkling Burgundy'** bears wine-colored flowers; and **'Yuletide'** has single, red flowers with bright yellow centers.

Features: upright to spreading shrub or small tree; colorful flowers; foliage
Height: 18"–20', sometimes to 50'
Spread: 3–12' **Hardiness:** zones 7–9

Cedar

Cedrus

A mature cedar tree, with its tow-ering form and elegant, layered, sweeping branches, is truly a magnificent sight to behold. Do not confuse the 'true cedars' (*Cedrus*) with the native arborvitae (*Thuja*), which we commonly refer to as 'cedar.'

Growing

Cedars grow well in **full sun** or **partial shade**. The soil can be of any type as long as it is **well drained**. A **moist, loamy** soil of **average to high fertility** is preferable.

Tips

Cedars are very large trees, best suited to large properties and parks.

Recommended

C. atlantica (atlas cedar, blue atlas cedar) is a large, wide-spreading, pyramidal tree with branches that sweep the ground. Smaller cultivars are available. **'Glauca Pendula'** is an interesting cultivar with trailing branches. (Zones 6–8)

C. deodara (deodar cedar) is the largest and fastest growing cedar, but it is not very cold hardy. Cultivars more reasonable in size are often more tolerant of winter temperatures. (Zones 7–8)

C. lebani (cedar of Lebanon) is often too big for the home garden, but it has cultivars that suit space-restricted settings. (Zones 5–7)

C. deodara (above), C. atlantica (below)

C. lebani *is depicted on the national flag of Lebanon.*

Features: large, upright, spreading or pendulous, evergreen tree; foliage; cones; bark **Height:** 3–130' **Spread:** 15–40' **Hardiness:** zones 5–8

Crape Myrtle
Lagerstroemia

L. indica cultivars (above & below)

C rape myrtle offers a unique element to just about any setting and requires little care.

Growing
Crape myrtle performs best in **full sun** but tolerates light shade. It likes **well-drained, neutral to slightly acidic** soil.

Once established, crape myrtle is quite drought tolerant, but does best with an occasional deep watering. Do not water from overhead.

Tips
Crape myrtles make excellent specimens. *L. indica* can be used for street trees and in lawns. The shrubs can be used for hedging, screening, and shrub borders and in mass plantings. Select plants carefully when underplanting around crape myrtle—the roots are quite competitive.

Recommended
L. fauriei (Japanese crape myrtle) is a medium-sized tree with erect, outward-arching branches. It bears lush green leaves, attractive bark and small, white flower clusters. Many cultivars exist, including '**Fantasy**' that produces bark showier than the species, a vase-like form and white flowers.

L. indica is a multi-stemmed, small tree. All summer it bears clusters of ruffled, crepe-like flowers in white and shades of red, pink or purple. The bronze-tinged, light green foliage turns dark glossy green in summer and yellow, orange or red in fall. The gray-brown bark exfoliates to reveal pinkish bark. Both standard and dwarf varieties are available, in varied sizes and flower colors. '**Carolina Beauty**' has dark red flower clusters and leaves that turn orange in fall. '**Natchez**' is a vigorous grower, bearing white flowers and is rarely affected by powdery mildew.

Features: flower clusters in shades of white, pink, red, purple, coral; exfoliating bark; fall color **Height:** 8–30' **Spread:** 6–16' **Hardiness:** zones 7–9

Cryptomeria
Cryptomeria

What would a southern garden be without the graceful addition of a tall, evergreen specimen such as this? With so much to offer year-round, cryptomeria is a must-have tree.

Growing
Cryptomeria prefers **full sun to light shade**. The soil should be **fertile, well drained, rich** and **deep**. Plant cryptomeria higher in heavily clay-based soils, and lower in deeply soil-amended spaces. Mulch well to prevent drying out during periods of drought.

Tips
Tall conifers are often used as specimens in residential landscapes and gardens. They're also planted for screening.

Recommended
C. japonica is a vigorous-growing tree with a slightly columnar habit and pendulous branches. The needle-like, bright green to bluish green leaves turn brown-purple as the days grow cooler. Attractive, thin, reddish brown bark peels off the trunk and branches. **'Benjamin Franklin'** produces foliage that remains green year-round and is highly tolerant to wind and salt. It will grow into a tall tree form. **'Black Dragon'** bears light green foliage that darkens to almost black in fall. It grows slowly, only 5' tall and 7' wide over a 10-year period. **'Elegans'** is grayish green in color but turns a coppery red in winter. It can grow quite tall and wide. **'Pygmaea'** is a dwarf selection that grows 1–2' wide and tall, and **'Yoshino'** is similar to the species but smaller in size.

Features: conical, columnar, coniferous tree or shrub; large; evergreen foliage; winter color; form **Height:** 1–100' **Spread:** 1–30' **Hardiness:** zones 6–8

C. japonica 'Benjamin Franklin' (above)
C. japonica 'Radicans' (below)

Dogwood
Cornus

C. florida 'Cherokee Chief' (above)
C. kousa var. chinensis (below)

Whether your garden is wet, dry, sunny or shaded, there is a dogwood for almost every condition.

Growing
Dogwoods grow equally well in **full sun, light shade** or **partial shade**, with a slight preference for light shade. The soil should be of **average to high fertility, high in organic matter, neutral** or **slightly acidic** and **well drained**.

Tips
Shrub dogwoods can be included in a shrub or mixed border. They look best in groups rather than as single specimens. The tree species make wonderful specimen plants and are small enough to include in most gardens. Use them along the edge of a woodland, in a shrub or mixed border, at the side of a house, or near a pond, water feature or patio.

Recommended
C. florida (flowering dogwood) is a conical tree or shrub with slightly twisted or curled foliage that turns a brilliant red and purple in fall. Green flowers tipped with yellow and surrounded by white to pink bracts are borne in spring, followed by bright red fruit. Many cultivars are available with vivid flower colors and variegated leaves, including **'Cherokee Brave,'** bearing red bracts with white centers; **'Cherokee Princess,'** bearing white blooms; and **'Rubra,'** bearing pink or rose pink bracts.

C. kousa (Kousa dogwood) is grown for its flowers, fruit, fall color and interesting bark. The white-bracted flowers are followed by bright red fruit. The foliage turns red and purple in fall. **Var. chinensis** (Chinese dogwood) grows more vigorously and has larger flowers. The cultivar **'Satomi'** has soft, pink flowers.

Features: deciduous, large shrub or small tree; white, pink, ruby late-spring to early-summer flowers; fall foliage and fruit; stem color
Height: 5–30' **Spread:** 5–30'
Hardiness: zones 5–9

False Cypress
Chamaecyparis

C. pisifera 'Mops' (above), *C. pisifera* 'Squarrosa' (below)

Conifer shoppers are blessed with a marvelous selection of false cypresses that offers color, size, shape and growth habits not available in most other evergreens.

Growing
False cypress prefer **full sun to partial shade**. The soil should be **fertile, moist, neutral to acidic** and **well drained**. Alkaline soils are tolerated. In shaded areas, growth may be sparse or thin.

Tips
Tree varieties are used as specimen plants and for hedging. The dwarf and slow-growing cultivars are used in borders and rock gardens and as bonsai. False cypress shrubs can be grown near the house or as evergreen specimens in large containers.

Recommended
There are several available species of false cypress and many cultivars. The scaly foliage can be in a drooping or strand-like form, in fan-like or feathery sprays and may be dark green, bright green or yellow. Plant forms vary from mounding or rounded to tall and pyramidal, or narrow with pendulous branches. *C. obtusa* (Hinoki cypress) is a broad conical tree with dark green foliage and a mature size of up to 70'. Cultivars in much smaller forms include **'Nana Gracilis'** that grows 10' tall in a pyramidal form. *C. pisifera* (Sawara cypress) has an open habit and flattened sprays of bright green foliage. The species grows up to 70' tall and 15' wide. Cultivars include **'Filifera,'** bearing slender branches and dark green foliage, and **'Filifera Aurea,'** which bears golden yellow leaves and grows 40' tall. Check with your local garden center or nursery to see what is available.

Features: narrow, pyramidal, evergreen tree or shrub; attractive foliage; cones
Height: 2–70' **Spread:** 2–20'
Hardiness: zones 4–8

Firethorn

Pyracantha

P. coccinea (above), P. coccinea 'Teton' (below)

Firethorn is a winner with its ability to be care-free and to act as both a groundcover and a hedge.

Growing

Firethorn prefers **full sun** but tolerates partial shade, though it does not fruit as heavily in partial shade. The soil should be **rich, moist** and **well drained**. Well-established plants tolerate dry soil. Shelter plants from strong winds. Firethorn resents being moved once established and requires some pruning to keep it looking neat and attractive.

Tips

Despite its potential for rampant growth, firethorn has a wide variety of uses. It is often used for formal or informal hedges and barriers because of the abundant prickles. Firethorn can be grown as a large, informal shrub in naturalized gardens and borders, or as a climber if tied to a support. The low-growing, spreading types make colorful groundcovers.

Recommended

P. coccinea is a large, spiny shrub that grows 8–12' tall and wide, and bears scarlet fruit. Cultivars are available in varied forms and with bright orange berries. **Firethorn hybrids** are among the most colorful and hardy. **'Gnome'** grows 6–8' tall and wide, bearing orange berries throughout its densely branched form. **'Mohave'** grows 12' tall and produces orange-red berries. **'Red Elf'** grows 2' tall and wide, and bears dark green leaves and bright red fruit. **'Ruby Mound'** produces long, arching branches in a spreading form, growing 10' wide and 2' tall. **'Teton'** is an upright shrub 12-15' tall and 4-8' wide. The leaves are bright green and the fruit is yellow-orange. It is resistant to both fireblight and scab.

Features: dense, thorny, evergreen or semi-evergreen shrub; foliage; flowers; late-summer and fall fruit **Height:** 2–15' **Spread:** 2–15' **Hardiness:** zones 6–10

Flowering Crabapple
Malus

Loads of spring flowers, a brilliant display of colorful autumn fruit and exceptional winter hardiness—what more could anyone ask from a small, flowering tree?

Growing

Flowering crabapples prefer **full sun** but tolerate partial shade. The soil should be of **average to rich fertility, moist** and **well drained**. These trees tolerate damp soil but suffer in wet locations.

Tips

Flowering crabapples make excellent specimen plants. Many varieties are quite small, so there is one to suit almost any size of garden. Some forms are even small enough to grow in large containers.

Crabapples' flexible, young branches make these trees good choices to create espalier specimens along a wall or fence.

Recommended

There are hundreds of crabapples available. When choosing a species, variety or cultivar, one of the most important attributes to look for is disease resistance. Even the most beautiful flowers, fruit or habit will never look good if the plant is ravaged by pests or diseases. Ask for information about new, resistant cultivars at your local nursery or garden center.

Features: rounded, mounded or spreading, small to medium, deciduous tree; attractive spring flowers in shades of white, pink, purple-red, red; late-season and winter fruit; fall foliage; bark **Height:** 5–30' **Spread:** 6–30' **Hardiness:** zones 4–8

Forsythia
Forsythia

F. x intermedia (above & below)

Forsythias can be used as hedging plants, but they look most attractive and flower best when grown informally.

These shrubs are treated a bit like relatives. It's fabulous to see them when they burst into bloom after a long, dreary winter, but they just seem to take up garden space once they are done flowering. The introduction of new selections with more decorative foliage has made them more appealing.

Growing

Forsythias grow best in **full sun** but some selections tolerate or prefer light or partial shade. The soil should be of **average fertility, moist** and **well drained**. These plants are more cold hardy than their flower buds. In a sheltered spot, or if covered by snow for the winter, forsythias may flower in a colder than recommended hardiness zone.

Tips

These shrubs are gorgeous while in flower but most aren't very interesting for the rest of the year. However, new selections with decorative foliage are being introduced to the market each year. Include forsythias in a shrub or mixed border where other flowering plants will provide interest once the forsythias' early-season glory has passed.

Recommended

F. x *intermedia* is a large shrub with upright stems that arch as they mature. It grows 5–10' tall and spreads 5–12'. Bright yellow flowers emerge in early to mid-spring, before the leaves. Many cultivars are available. A few of the better selections include GOLD TIDE, **'Lynwood Gold'** and **'Spring Glory.'**

Features: spreading, deciduous shrub with upright or arching branches; attractive, early to mid-spring yellow flowers **Height:** 2–10' **Spread:** 3–15' **Hardiness:** zones 5–8

Fothergilla
Fothergilla

$\mathcal{F}$lowers, fragrance, fall color and interesting soft tan to brownish stems give fothergillas year-round appeal.

Growing
Fothergilla grows equally well in **full sun** or **partial shade,** but these plants bear the most flowers and have the best fall color in full sun. The soil should be of **average fertility, acidic, humus rich, moist** and **well drained.**

Tips
Fothergilla is attractive and useful in shrub or mixed borders, in woodland gardens and when combined with ever-green groundcover.

Recommended
F. gardenii (dwarf fothergilla) is a bushy shrub that bears fragrant, white flowers. The foliage turns yellow, orange or red in fall. It grows 2–3' tall with an equal spread but can grow taller. Cultivars are available, including '**Blue Mist,**' which produces bluish foliage throughout the growing season.

F. major (large fothergilla) is a larger, rounded shrub that bears fragrant, white flowers. The autumn colors are yellow, orange or scarlet. This species can grow 8' tall and 6' wide. '**Blue Shadow**' is an exceptional new cultivar with attractive blue foliage. '**Mount Airy**' is a smaller selection with dark green foliage that turns shades of yellow, orange or scarlet in fall.

F. major (above & below)

The bottlebrush-shaped flowers of fothergilla have a delicate, honey scent. The shrubs are generally problem free and make wonderful companions to azaleas, rhododendrons and other acid-loving, woodland plants.

Features: dense, rounded or bushy, deciduous shrub; fragrant, white, spring flowers; fall foliage
Height: 2–8' **Spread:** 3–6'
Hardiness: zones 4–9

Fringe Tree
Chionanthus

C. virginicus (above & below)

Fringe trees adapt to a wide range of growing conditions. They are cold hardy and in spring are densely covered in silky, white, honey-scented flowers that shimmer in the wind.

Growing
Fringe trees prefer **full sun**. They do best in soil that is **fertile, acidic, moist** and **well drained** but adapt to most soil conditions. In the wild they are often found growing alongside stream banks.

Tips
Fringe trees work well as specimen plants, as part of a border or beside a water feature. These plants begin flowering at a very early age.

Recommended
C. retusus (Chinese fringe tree) is a rounded, spreading shrub or small tree with deeply furrowed, peeling bark and erect, fragrant, white flower clusters. (Zones 5–9)

C. virginicus (white fringe tree) is a spreading, small tree or large shrub that bears drooping, fragrant, white flowers.

Features: rounded or spreading, deciduous, large shrub or small tree; fragrant, white early-summer flowers; bark **Height:** 10–25'
Spread: 10–25' **Hardiness:** zones 4–9

Glossy Abelia
Abelia

A. x *grandiflora* (above & below)

This vigorous shrub is covered with pink buds in spring that open to white, creating a wonderful display.

Growing

Glossy abelia grows well in **full sun** or **partial shade**. The soil should be **fertile**, relatively **moist** and **well drained**. Some pruning is required right after flowering to keep it full and tidy.

Tips

Glossy abelia makes a lovely addition to a shrub or mixed border. Because it is a relatively large shrub, it is best suited for the back of the border.

Recommended

A.* x *grandiflora is a rounded, evergreen or semi-evergreen shrub with arching branches covered in dark green, glossy foliage. Funnel-shaped flowers are borne in mid-summer and continue to emerge until fall. The flowers are fragrant and white in color but touched with a hint of pink. Cultivars are available with yellow and green-marked foliage or solid foliage.

Branches can be cut and brought in the house just before the flower buds open to make a wonderfully fragrant spring bouquet.

Features: rounded to upright semi-evergreen shrub; glossy foliage; orange to red fall foliage; white spring flowers **Height:** 6–10' **Spread:** 4–6' **Hardiness:** zones 4–8

Glossy Privet
Ligustrum

L. japonicum (above & below)

Glossy privets are among the most-used hedge plants in the South.

Growing
Glossy privets grow equally well in **full sun** or **partial shade**. They adapt to any well-drained soil and tolerate polluted and urban conditions.

Hedges can be pruned twice every summer. Plants grown in borders or as specimens should be kept neat by removing up to one-third of the mature growth each year.

Tips
Glossy privets are commonly grown as hedges because they are fast growing, adaptable and inexpensive. Left unpruned, a privet becomes a large shrub with arching branches. This form looks quite attractive, especially when blooming.

Recommended
L. japonicum (Japanese privet) is an evergreen shrub with a dense, compact growth habit. It can grow to 10–12' tall and spread to 8'. It bears roundish oval leaves that are dark green, with glossy uppersides and pale undersides. White, fragrant flower clusters are produced from midsummer to fall, followed by black fruit. Many cultivars are available in various forms, including **'Recurvifolium,'** a slower-growing selection with rounded, leathery foliage and a mature size that is less than half that of the species.

L. lucidum (glossy privet) is an evergreen tree that grows 35–40' tall and wide. It is a round-headed tree with leathery leaves and large, feathery clusters of fragrant flowers, followed by black fruit. This species is more often grown as a tree specimen.

Features: upright or arching, deciduous or semi-evergreen shrub or tree; adaptability; fast and dense growth **Height:** 4–40'
Spread: 4–40' **Hardiness:** zones 3–8

Golden Rain Tree

Koelreuteria

K. paniculata (above & below)

With its delicate clusters of yellow flowers and overall lacy appearance in summer, this lovely tree deserves wider use as a specimen or shade tree.

Growing

Golden rain tree grows best in **full sun**. The soil should be **average to fertile, moist** and **well drained**. This tree can tolerate heat, drought, wind and air pollution. It also adapts to most pH levels and is fast growing.

Tips

Golden rain tree makes an excellent shade or specimen tree for small properties. Its ability to adapt to a wide range of soils makes it useful in many situations. The fruit is not messy and will not stain a patio or deck if planted to shade these areas.

Recommended

K. paniculata is an attractive, rounded, spreading tree. It bears long clusters of small, yellow flowers in mid-summer, followed by red-tinged, green capsular fruit. The leaves are attractive and somewhat lacy in appearance. The foliage may turn bright yellow in fall. Cultivars are available, including **'Fastigiata,'** which grows 25' tall but only 3' wide, and **'Rose Lantern,'** bearing rose pink decorative capsules at the end of summer.

This Asian species is one of the few trees with yellow flowers and one of the only trees to bloom in mid- or late summer.

Features: rounded, spreading, deciduous tree; attractive foliage; fruit; mid- or late-summer yellow flowers **Height:** 25–40' **Spread:** 3–40' **Hardiness:** zones 5–8

Holly
Ilex

I. opaca (above), *I. hybrid* (below)

ollies vary greatly in shape and size and can be such delights when placed with full consideration for their needs.

Growing

Hollies prefer **full sun** but tolerate partial shade. The soil should be of **average to rich fertility, humus rich** and **moist**. Hollies perform best in **acidic** soil with a pH of 6.5 or lower. Shelter them from winter wind to prevent the evergreen leaves from drying out. Apply a summer mulch to keep the roots cool and moist.

Tips

Hollies can be used in groups, in woodland gardens and in shrub and mixed borders. They can also be shaped into hedges. Winterberry is good for naturalizing in moist sites.

Recommended

There is an unending supply of hollies, and most selections are worthy of growing in southern gardens. Consult your local garden center for their best recommendations.

I. cornuta (Chinese holly) is an evergreen shrub or small tree that is very tolerant of excessive heat. *I. hybrids* offer every form, size and special characteristic available, including broad, pyramidal forms, colorful berries, dwarf selections and leaves so dark they appear to be almost black. *I. opaca* (American holly) grows 40–50' tall but takes a lifetime to get there, and offers hundreds of cultivars with unique qualities. *I. verticillata* (winterberry, winterberry holly) is a deciduous, native species grown for its explosion of red, orange or yellow fruit that persists into winter. *I. vomitoria* is often used as tall, dense hedging material, and is tolerant of a coastal environment.

Features: erect or spreading, evergreen or deciduous shrub or tree; attractive, glossy, sometimes spiny, foliage; fruit **Height:** 3–50' **Spread:** 3–40' **Hardiness:** zones 3–9

Hydrangea
Hydrangea

ydrangeas have many attractive qualities, including showy, often long-lasting flowers and glossy green leaves, some of which turn beautiful colors in fall.

Growing

Hydrangeas grow well in **full sun** or **partial shade**, but some species tolerate full shade. Shade or partial shade reduces leaf and flower scorch in hotter gardens. The soil should be of **average to high fertility, humus rich, moist** and **well drained**. These plants perform best in cool, moist conditions.

Tips

Hydrangeas can be included in shrub or mixed borders, used as specimens or informal barriers and planted in groups or containers.

Recommended

H. arborescens (smooth hydrangea) is a rounded shrub that flowers well, even in shady conditions. Superior selections include '**Annabelle**' and WHITE DOME.

H. macrophylla (bigleaf hydrangea, garden hydrangea) is a large, rounded shrub with large, shiny, dark green leaves and lacecap flowerheads of red, blue, pink or white. The many cultivars can have either hortensia or lacecap flowerheads. The species and cultivars bloom on older wood.

H. paniculata (panicle hydrangea) is a spreading to upright, large shrub or small tree that bears white flowers from late summer to early fall. '**Grandiflora**'

H. quercifolia (above), *H. macrophylla* cultivars (below)

(Peegee hydrangea) is a commonly available cultivar. Other excellent selections include LIMELIGHT, '**Little Lamb**' and '**Pink Diamond**.'

H. quercifolia (oakleaf hydrangea) is a mound-forming shrub with cinnamon brown, exfoliating bark, large leaves that are lobed like an oak's and turn bronze to bright red in fall, and conical clusters of sterile and fertile flowers. Cultivars include '**Little Honey**,' '**Pee Wee**,' '**Snowflake**' and '**Snow Queen**.'

Features: deciduous, mounding or spreading shrub or tree; flowers in shades of purple, red, pink, white, blue; foliage; bark **Height:** 3–22' **Spread:** 3–15' **Hardiness:** zones 4–9

Japanese Aucuba
Aucuba

A. japonica cultivars (above & below)

This tough plant is tolerant of frost, deep shade, pollution, neglect and salty, windy coastal conditions. The foliage and berries are a dynamic addition to any garden.

Growing

Japanese aucuba grows well in **partial to full shade** in **moderately fertile, humus-rich, moist, well-drained** soil. Plants with variegated foliage show the best leaf color in partial shade. This plant adapts to most soil conditions as long as the soil is not waterlogged, and it tolerates urban pollution.

Tips

Japanese aucuba can be used in deeply shaded locations where no other plants will grow, such as under the canopy of larger trees. It can also be used as a specimen, in a large planter and as a hedge or screen.

Generally, both a male and female plant must be present for the females to set fruit. The fruits are not edible.

Recommended

A. japonica 'Nana' is a compact plant with erect stems, a neatly rounded habit and glossy green leaves. It grows 3–4' tall and wide. Female plants develop red berries in fall. The fruit is highly visible as it is held above the foliage. Many cultivars of *A. japonica* are available and are usually developed for their variegated foliage. The species is twice the size of 'Nana.'

Also called: dwarf Japanese aucuba
Features: bushy, rounded, evergreen shrub; foliage; fruit; adaptability **Height:** 3–4'
Spread: 3–4' **Hardiness:** zones 7–10

Japanese Zelkova

Zelkova

Japanese zelkova not only has an attractive form, it boasts elegant, clean, rich green foliage. In autumn, the leaves develop rich hues of yellow, orange, red or purple. With time, the bark matures into a pleasing patchwork of gray and brown.

Growing

Japanese zelkova grows well in **full sun** or **partial shade**. The soil should be **fertile, humus rich, moist** and **well drained**. Young trees are sensitive to wind, drought and cold, but established plants tolerate these conditions. Prune Japanese zelkova in fall or winter to encourage neat, even growth.

Tips

Japanese zelkova is a medium-sized tree with an attractive habit and foliage. It is well suited as a residential shade tree or for street plantings.

Recommended

Z. serrata grows 50–80' tall or more, with an equal spread. It is vase-shaped when young and develops a broader, more spreading habit and exfoliating bark as it matures. Inconspicuous flowers are produced in early spring. The dark green leaves turn yellow or orange, and sometimes red in fall. **'Green Vase'** has a vase-shaped habit and develops a strong, straight trunk. It grows up to 70' tall and spreads up to 50'. **'Village**

Z. serrata 'Village Green'(above & below)

Green' is a hardy, fast-growing, pest- and disease-resistant tree. It develops red fall color.

The mature, exfoliating bark of Japanese zelkova provides interest in the winter landscape.

Features: vase-shaped to broadly spreading, deciduous tree; summer and fall foliage
Height: 50–80' or more **Spread:** 50–80'
Hardiness: zones 5–9

Juneberry
Amelanchier

A. alnifolia 'Regent' (above)

The *Amelanchier* species are first-rate North American natives, bearing lacy, white flowers in spring, followed by edible berries. In fall, the foliage color ranges from glowing apricot to deep red.

Growing

Juneberries grow well in **full sun** or **light shade**. They prefer **acidic** soil that is **fertile, humus rich, moist** and **well drained**. They adjust to drought.

Tips

Juneberries make beautiful specimen plants or even shade trees in small gardens. The shrubbier forms can be grown along the edges of a woodland or in a border. In the wild these trees are often found growing near water sources and are beautiful beside ponds or streams.

Recommended

Several species and hybrids are available. *A. alnifolia* (serviceberry, Saskatoon) is a native shrub with white flowers and edible blue-black fruit. *A. arborea* (Juneberry) has a narrow tree form with larger clusters of white flowers compared to other species, resulting in more dark red to purple fruit. *A. x grandiflora* (apple serviceberry) is a small, spreading, often multi-stemmed tree. The new foliage is often a bronze color, turning green in summer and bright orange or red in fall. White spring flowers are followed by edible purple fruit in summer. **'Autumn Brilliance'** produces strong stems clothed in green leaves that change to a stunning orange-red in fall, and **'Prince William'** is a shrubby selection with great fall color.

Also called: downy serviceberry
Features: single- or multi-stemmed, deciduous, large shrub or small tree; white spring or early-summer flowers; edible fruit; fall color; bark
Height: 15–25' **Spread:** 15–20'
Hardiness: zones 3–8

Juniper
Juniperus

There may be a juniper in every gardener's future with all the choices available, from low, creeping plants to upright pyramidal forms.

Growing

Junipers prefer **full sun** but tolerate light shade. Ideally, the soil should be of **average fertility** and **well drained**, but these plants tolerate most conditions.

Tips

With the wide variety of junipers available, there are endless uses for them in the garden. They make prickly barriers and hedges, and they can be used in borders, as specimens or in groups. The larger species can be used to form windbreaks, while the low-growing species can be used in rock gardens and as groundcover.

Recommended

Junipers vary, not just from species to species, but often within a species. Cultivars are available for all species and may differ significantly from the species. **J. chinensis** (Chinese juniper) is a conical tree or spreading shrub. **J. conferta** and **J. horizontalis** (creeping juniper) are prostrate, creeping groundcovers. **J. davurica** and **J. procumbens** (Japanese garden juniper) are both wide-spreading, stiff-branched, low shrubs. **J. scopulorum** (Rocky Mountain juniper) can be upright, rounded, weeping or spreading. **J. squamata** (singleseed juniper) forms a prostrate or low, spreading shrub or a small, upright tree. **J. virginiana** (eastern redcedar) is a durable, upright or wide-spreading tree.

J. virginiana 'Blue Arrow' (above)
J. conferta 'Emerald Sea' (below)

It is a good idea to wear long sleeves and gloves when handling junipers as the prickly foliage gives some gardeners a rash. Juniper berries are poisonous if eaten in large quantities.

Features: conical or columnar tree, or rounded or spreading shrub, or prostrate groundcover; evergreen **Height:** 4"–80' **Spread:** 1–25' **Hardiness:** zones 3–9

Laurustinus

Viburnum

V. plicatum var. tomentosum 'Mariesii' (above)
V. plicatum var. tomentosum (below)

Good fall color, attractive form, shade tolerance, scented flowers and attractive fruit put laurustinus in a class by itself.

Growing

Laurustinus grows well in **full sun, partial shade** or **light shade**. The soil should be of **average fertility, moist** and **well**

drained. Laurustinus tolerates both alkaline and acidic soils.

These plants look neatest if deadheaded, but this practice prevents fruits from forming. Fruiting is better when more than one plant of a species is grown.

Tips

Laurustinus can be used in borders and woodland gardens. It is a good choice for plantings near swimming pools.

Recommended

Many *Viburnum* species, hybrids and cultivars are available.

V. carlesii (Korean spice viburnum) is a dense, bushy, rounded, deciduous shrub with white or pink, spice-scented flowers.

V. plicatum var. *tomentosum* (double-file viburnum) has a graceful, horizontal branching pattern that gives the shrub a layered effect, and lacy-looking, white flower clusters. Cultivars are available with varied forms, sizes and flower colors.

V. tinus (Laurustinus) is an evergreen species that grows 6–12' tall but spreads only half as wide. The newest foliage is wine colored but turns dark green as it matures. Pink buds emerge in tight clusters during winter, opening into white, lightly scented blossoms. Clusters of blue berries follow after the flowers. Cultivars are available in smaller sizes and with a higher resistance to mildew.

Features: bushy or spreading, evergreen, semi-evergreen or deciduous shrub; attractive, white or pink flowers (some fragrant); summer and fall foliage; fruit **Height:** 4–15' **Spread:** 4–15' **Hardiness:** zones 4–10

Leyland Cypress

x *Cupressocyparis*

x *C. leylandii*

Leyland cypress immediately invokes visions of evergreen privacy screening. Introduced in the mid-1970s, these evergreen trees have carved out a deep niche in the Virginia landscape.

Growing

Leyland cypress prefers growing in fully open and **sunny** locations but tolerates partial shade. **Moist** but **well drained** soils are best.

Tips

Leyland cypress is often used in evergreen privacy screens. It's equally as stunning and useful when planted as a single specimen or in small naturalistic groupings.

Recommended

x *Cupressocyparis leylandii* is the result of crossing *Cupressus macrocarpa* or cypress and *Chamaecyparis nootkatensis* or false cypress. This hybrid closely resembles both, displaying the best attributes of each genus. It is often topped or pruned to keep its tall form in check. The long, slender branches grow upright, clothed in gray-green, evergreen, flattened foliage sprays.

Leyland cypress is subject to overplanting in certain regions of the South; it should only be used when low numbers are present in your neighborhood. This practice will lend to its long-term survival and conservation.

Features: coniferous tree; dense and tall evergreen foliage; uses **Height:** 60–70'
Spread: 15–20' **Hardiness:** zones 6–9

Lilac

Syringa

S. meyeri (above), S. vulgaris (below)

The hardest thing about growing lilacs is choosing from the many species and hundreds of cultivars available.

Growing

Lilacs grow best in **full sun**. They prefer a slightly **alkaline or neutral** soil that is **fertile, humus rich** and **well drained**. These plants tolerate open, windy locations.

Tips

Include lilacs in a shrub or mixed border or use them to create an informal hedge. Japanese tree lilac can be used as a specimen tree.

Recommended

S. meyeri '**Palibin**' (Palibin lilac) is a compact, rounded shrub that bears fragrant, pink or lavender flowers. (Zones 3–7)

S. patula '**Miss Kim**' is a dwarf, compact lilac with pale purple flower buds that open lavender blue. It shows attractive, dark green foliage and vigorous growth. (Zones 3–7)

S. reticulata (Japanese tree lilac) is a rounded, large shrub or small tree that bears white flowers. '**Ivory Silk**' has a more compact habit and produces more flowers than the species. (Zones 3–7)

S. vulgaris (French lilac, common lilac) is the plant most people think of when they think of lilacs. It is a suckering, spreading shrub with an irregular habit that bears fragrant, lilac-colored flowers. Hundreds of cultivars with a variety of flower colors are available.

Lilacs are frost-loving shrubs that won't flower at all in the warm, southern parts of the U.S.

Features: rounded or suckering, deciduous shrub or small tree; attractive, lilac, white, purple, pink, lavender late-spring to mid-summer flowers **Height:** 3–30' **Spread:** 3–25' **Hardiness:** zones 2–8

London Planetree

Platanus

*L*ondon planetree produces a most interesting bark, which peels off in irregular patches, revealing different shades of color as the tree matures. That feature, and the tree's ability to survive the worst urban pollution, makes it a popular choice for lining streets in cities around the world.

Growing

London planetree grows well in **full sun**. Any soil conditions are tolerated. This tree thrives even in compacted soil with poor air circulation. The roots can lift and damage pavement, so plant this tree away from pavement edges.

Pruning is rarely required. London planetree, however, withstands heavy pruning and can be used as a very large hedge.

Tips

This large tree is best suited to parks, streetsides and spacious gardens.

Recommended

P. x *acerifolia* is a large tree with wide, spreading branches. It is grown for its tolerance of adverse conditions and its attractive, exfoliating bark. The flaking patches leave the smooth bark mottled with different colors. In fall, the leaves turn golden brown. **'Bloodgood'** is a popular, quick-growing, drought-tolerant cultivar that has some resistance to anthracnose. **'Columbia'** and **'Liberty'** are both resistant to disease and are attractive in habit and form.

P. x *acerifolia* (above & below)

London planetree is the dominant street and park tree in London, England, hence the common name.

Features: broad, rounded or pyramidal, deciduous tree; bark; foliage **Height:** 70–100'
Spread: 65–80 **Hardiness:** zones 4–8

Magnolia
Magnolia

M. x soulangeana (above & below)

Magnolias are beautiful, fragrant, versatile plants that also provide attractive winter structure.

Growing
Magnolias grow well in **full sun** or **partial shade**. The soil should be **fertile, humus rich, acidic, moist** and **well drained**. A summer mulch will help keep the roots cool and the soil moist.

Tips
Magnolias are used as specimen trees and the smaller species can be used in borders.

Avoid planting magnolias where the morning sun will encourage the blooms to open too early in the season. Cold, wind and rain can damage the blossoms.

Recommended
Many species, hybrids and cultivars in a range of sizes and with differing flowering times and flower colors are available. Three of the most common are *M. grandiflora* (Southern magnolia), a classic tree form that can grow 80' tall; *M. hybrids*, which are plentiful and offer almost every form and color imaginable; and *M. x soulangeana* (saucer magnolia), which is a rounded, spreading, deciduous shrub or tree with pink, purple or white flowers.

Features: upright to spreading, deciduous shrub or tree; white, pink, purple, yellow, cream, apricot flowers; fruit; foliage; bark
Height: 8–80' **Spread:** 5–30'
Hardiness: zones 4–8

Maple

Acer

Maples are attractive all year, with delicate flowers in spring, attractive foliage and hanging samaras in summer, vibrant leaf color in fall, and interesting bark and branch structures in winter.

Growing

Generally, maples do well in **full sun** or **light shade**, though this varies from species to species. The soil should be **fertile, moist, high in organic matter** and **well drained**.

Tips

Maples can be used as specimen trees, as large elements in shrub or mixed borders or as hedges. Some are useful as understory plants bordering wooded areas; others can be grown in containers on patios or terraces. Few Japanese gardens are without the attractive, smaller maples. Almost all maples can be used to create bonsai specimens.

Recommended

Maples are some of the most popular trees used as shade or street trees. Many are very large when fully mature, but there are also a few smaller species that are useful in smaller gardens, including **A. campestre** (hedge maple), **A. ginnala** (amur maple), **A. griseum** (paperbark maple), **A. japonicum** (full-moon maple), **A. palmatum** (Japanese maple) and **A. rubrum** (red maple). Check with your local nursery or garden center for availability.

A. palmatum cultivars (above & below)

Features: small, multi-stemmed, deciduous tree or large shrub; foliage; bark; winged fruit; fall color; form; inconspicuous greenish yellow flowers **Height:** 6–80' **Spread:** 6–70' **Hardiness:** zones 2–8

Mountain Laurel

Kalmia

K. latifolia 'Kaliedoscope' (above)
K. latifolia 'Fresca' (below)

You'll find yourself stopping cold to look at the large, colorful flower clusters produced by this underutilized shrub, which requires little more than a shaded location and an appreciation for beautiful flowers.

Growing

Mountain laurel prefers **light** or **partial shade**. The soil should be of **average to high fertility, moist, acidic** and **well drained**. Mountain laurel does not perform well in alkaline soil. A mulch of leaf mold or pine needles will keep the roots of this drought-sensitive plant from drying out.

Little pruning is required, but spent flowerheads can be removed in summer and awkward shoots removed as needed.

Tips

Use mountain laurel in a shaded part of a shrub or mixed border, in a woodland garden or combined with other acid- and shade-loving plants, such as rhododendrons. It makes a good container plant.

The flowers and foliage of mountain laurel are extremely **poisonous** and should not be consumed.

Recommended

K. latifolia (mountain laurel, calico bush) is a dense and bushy shrub with glossy, dark leaves. Large clusters of pale to deep pink, occasionally white, flowers emerge in late spring to mid-summer. The flower buds are also distinctive compared to other species as they appear 'crimped' toward the tip and are darker in color. Many cultivars are available, but **'Olympic Fire'** stands out. It bears wavy margined leaves, and large, pink clusters of flowers emerge from its red buds.

Features: large flower clusters in shades of white, pink, red, coral, bicolored, solid; form
Height: 3–10' **Spread:** 3–10'
Hardiness: zones 4–9

Myrica
Myrica

Myrica is a wonderful shrub that can stand alone as a specimen or blend easily into a mixed border. It can also be trained as a small tree.

Growing

Myrica grows well in **full sun** or **partial shade** and adapts to most soil conditions, from poor sandy soil to heavy clay soil. It tolerates salty conditions, making it useful in coastal conditions and where road spray and runoff occur.

Tips

Myrica forms large colonies and can be used for mass plantings and in under-used areas.

Recommended

M. cerifera (wax myrtle) is a rounded, deciduous shrub with an upright, branching habit. Inconspicuous flowers are produced in spring followed by waxy, gray fruit along the shoots. The fruit stays on the branches into the winter months. This species can grow 15' in height with an equal spread. (Zones 6–9)

M. pensylvanica (Northern Bayberry) is a large, upright shrub with a rounded, dense growth habit. It is especially well suited to coastal gardens, because of its tolerance to poor soil conditions and salt. This species is a suckering selection, bearing toothed, glossy foliage that carries a light scent. Inconspicuous flowers are produced in spring before the leaves emerge, followed by waxy, grayish white fruit that persists into winter. This species grows 9–10' tall and 5–12' wide.

M. cerifera (above & below)

The berries are often used in candle-making, hence the names 'bayberry' for its aromatic nature and 'wax myrtle' for its waxy fruit.

Features: interesting fruit; habit; semi-evergreen to evergreen, lush foliage. **Habit:** rounded, deciduous to semi-evergreen, evergreen shrub
Height: 9–15' **Spread:** 5–15'
Hardiness: zones 4–9

Nandina

Nandina

N. domestica (above), N. domestica 'Compacta' (below)

Nandina is also called 'heavenly bamboo,' because of the similarity of its foliage to bamboo foliage, though it is not a true relative of bamboo.

Growing

Nandina prefers **full sun to partial shade** in **humus-rich, moist, well-drained** soil. It is prone to chlorosis when planted in alkaline soils. It prefers regular water but can tolerate drier conditions. Shrubs in full sun that experience some frost produce the best fall and winter color.

Tips

Use nandina in shrub borders, as background plants, and as informal hedges and screens. It is a great plant for containers. Mass planting ensures a good quantity of the shiny, bright red berries.

Recommended

N. domestica produces clumps of thin, upright, lightly branched stems and fine-textured foliage. It grows 6–8' tall and 3–5' wide, and spreads slowly by suckering. It bears large, loose clusters of small, white flowers, followed by persistent, spherical fruit. New foliage is tinged bronze to red, becoming light to medium green in summer, with many varieties turning red to reddish purple in fall and winter. Many colorful, compact and dwarf cultivars are available, including **'Fire Power,'** which grows 2' tall and wide, with foliage tinted with red that intensifies in winter, and **'Nana Purpurea,'** which produces purplish green foliage that turns to bright red as the days grow cooler.

Also called: sacred bamboo, common nandina
Features: upright to rounded, evergreen or semi-evergreen shrub; white, late-spring to early-summer flowers; fruit; foliage; tough, long-lived **Height:** 18"–8' **Spread:** 18"–5'
Hardiness: zones 7–9

Oak

Quercus

The oak's classic shape, outstanding fall color, deep roots and long life are some of its many assets. Plant it for its individual beauty and for posterity.

Growing

Oaks grow well in **full sun** or **partial shade**. The soil should be **fertile, moist** and **well drained**. These trees can be difficult to establish; transplant them only when they are young.

Tips

Oaks are large trees that are best used as specimens or for groves in parks and large gardens. Do not disturb the ground around the base of an oak; this tree is very sensitive to changes in grade.

Recommended

There are many oaks to choose from. A few popular species are **Q. alba** (white oak), which is an oval-rounded tree with great fall color, growing 50–80' tall and wide; **Q. coccinea** (scarlet oak), noted for having the most brilliant red fall color of all the oaks; **Q. palustris** (pin oak), a vigorous, conical tree with pendent lower branches and deeply lobed leaves; **Q. phellos** (willow oak) is similar to *Q. palustris* in form and habit but bears willow-like foliage rather than the deeply lobed leaves most people are familiar with; **Q. rubra** (red oak), a rounded, spreading tree with fall color ranging from yellow to red-brown; and **Q. virginiana** (live oak), a massive, wide-spreading tree with reddish brown bark and leathery, small, dark green leaves. Some cultivars are available; check with your local nursery or garden center.

Features: large, rounded, spreading, deciduous tree; summer and fall foliage; bark; acorns **Height:** 35–120' **Spread:** 10–100' **Hardiness:** zones 3–9

Q. phellos (above), Q. virginiana (below)

Acorns are generally not edible, though acorns of certain oak species are edible but usually must be processed first to leach out the bitter tannins.

Osmanthus
Osmanthus

O. heterophyllus (above & below)

Osmanthus, also commonly known as tea olives, is the perfect complement to the winter garden. Fragrant flowers and evergreen foliage offer color and interest when little else is happening.

Growing

Osmanthus prefers to grow in a location with **full to partial sun**, **sheltered** from the winter sun and wind. The soil should be **fertile, well drained** and **neutral to acidic**.

Tips

Most osmanthus selections grow to be large shrubs that are ideal for tall privacy screens and hedges. Others are considered to be either large shrubs or small trees, depending on the application. Accepting of pruning, osmanthus is often trained as a small specimen tree for smaller yards and gardens and is perfect for naturalizing.

Recommended

O. heterophyllus (holly osmanthus) is a dense, rounded shrub with sharply toothed, holly-like foliage. Tubular, fragrant, white flowers are produced in late summer to fall, followed by bluish black fruit. Cultivars are available with yellow-margined, mottled and pink-tinged leaves. (Zones 7–9)

Many fragrances on the market have been scented with hints of osmanthus. The sweet scent is complemented by essence of lemon blossom and green apple.

Features: shiny, ornate foliage; form; white, orange, yellow, cream flowers **Height:** 8–20'
Spread: 6–10' **Hardiness:** zones 7–10

Pieris

Pieris

Need a shrub that doesn't lose its leaves or need pruning, blooms through spring and rarely has pest problems? *P. japonica* fits the bill and adds fragrance to the garden as a bonus.

Growing

Pieris grows equally well in **full sun** or **partial shade.** The soil should be of **average fertility, acidic, humus rich, moist** and **well drained.** Gardeners who are not in mild, coastal areas should ensure pieris has a sheltered location protected from the hot sun and drying winds.

Tips

Pieris can be used in a shrub or mixed border, in a woodland garden or as a specimen. Try grouping it with rhododendrons and other acid-loving plants.

Recommended

P. japonica bears white flowers in long, pendulous clusters at the ends of its branches. Several dwarf cultivars are available, as are cultivars with bright red new foliage, variegated foliage and pink flowers. **'Mountain Fire'** and **'Snowdrift'** are two fine examples for southern gardens.

P. japonica cultivars (above & below)

Pieris' flower buds form in late summer the year before it flowers. They provide an attractive show all winter long.

Also called: lily-of-the-valley shrub
Features: compact, rounded, evergreen shrub; colorful new growth; white late-winter to spring flowers **Height:** 3–12' **Spread:** 3–10'
Hardiness: zones 5–8

Pine

Pinus

P. mugo (above), P. strobus (below)

Pines offer exciting possibilities for any garden. Exotic-looking pines are available with soft or stiff needles, needles with yellow bands, trunks with patterned or mother-of-pearl-like bark and varied forms.

Growing

Pines grow best in **full sun**. These trees adapt to most **well-drained** soils but do not tolerate polluted urban conditions.

Tips

Pines can be used as specimen trees, as hedges or to create windbreaks. Smaller cultivars can be included in shrub or mixed borders. These trees are not heavy feeders; fertilizing encourages rapid new growth that is weak and susceptible to pest and disease problems.

To keep low-growing pines more compact, pinch up to half of the new growth each spring.

Recommended

There are many available pines, both trees and shrubby dwarf plants. *P. bungeana* (lace-bark pine) grows 50–75' tall and 30–50' wide. It matures into an open, spreading specimen with dull, gray bark that peels similar to a sycamore tree's. *P. mugo* is a shrub species that grows 4–8' tall and 8–15' wide. Dwarf cultivars are available that grow to half the height and width of the species. *P. strobus* (white pine, eastern white pine) is a tall specimen, growing 50–80' in height and 20–40' in width. It is a symmetrical tree with a pyramidal habit and horizontal branching. Many cultivars are available. *P. taeda* (loblolly pine) also grows quite tall with an open-crowned, mature form. Check with your local garden center or nursery to find out what other selections are available.

Features: upright, columnar or spreading, evergreen tree; foliage; bark; cones
Height: 4–80' Spread: 6–50'
Hardiness: zones 2–8

Prunus

Prunus

Cherries are so beautiful and uplifting after the gray days of winter that few gardeners can resist them.

Growing

These flowering fruit trees prefer **full sun**. The soil should be of **average fertility, moist** and **well drained**. Shallow roots emerge from the lawn if the tree is not getting sufficient water.

Tips

Prunus species are beautiful as specimen plants and many are small enough to be included in almost any garden. Smaller species and cultivars can also be included in borders or grouped to form informal hedges or barriers.

Recommended

The following are a few popular selections from the many species, hybrids and cultivars available. Check with your local nursery or garden center for other selections. *P. cerasifera* (cherry plum) is a rounded, deciduous tree with dark foliage and white flowers that are followed by plum-like, red or yellow fruit. Cultivars include **'Thundercloud'** that bears pink flowers and purple foliage. *P. laurocerasus* (cherry laurel) is a dense, bushy shrub with glossy leaves and fragrant, white flowers. Cultivars are available, including **'Otto Uyken,'** a compact cultivar, and *P.* **'Okame,'** which is a bushy tree or shrub with dark green foliage that turns bright orange-red in fall and bears carmine red blossoms in early

P. 'Okame' (above)

spring. *P. serrulata* is a rounded tree with peeling, glossy, copper bark, white spring flowers and great fall color. *P.* x *yedoensis* (potomac cherry, yoshino cherry) is a large, spreading tree with arching branches, dark green leaves and pale pink flowers in early spring. Cultivars are available with varied pink blossoms and weeping habits.

Features: upright, rounded, spreading or weeping deciduous tree or shrub; attractive, pink or white spring to early-summer flowers; fruit; bark; fall foliage **Height:** 4–75' **Spread:** 4–50' **Hardiness:** zones 2–8

Redbud
Cercis

Redbud is an outstanding treasure of spring. Deep magenta flowers bloom before the leaves emerge, and their impact is intense. As the buds open, the flowers turn pink, covering the long, thin branches in pastel clouds.

Growing
Redbud grows well in **full sun, partial shade** or **light shade**. The soil should be a **fertile, deep loam** that is **moist** and **well drained**. This plant has tender roots and does not like being transplanted.

Tips
Redbud can be used as a specimen tree, in a shrub or mixed border or in a woodland garden.

Recommended
C. canadensis (eastern redbud) is a spreading, multi-stemmed tree that bears red, purple or pink flowers. The young foliage is bronze, fading to green over the summer and turning bright yellow in fall. The species grows 30' tall and wide. Many beautiful cultivars are available, including **'Alba'** that has white blossoms, and **'Forest Pansy'** that bears dramatic, dark red-purple leaves.

C. canadensis (above & below)

Redbud is not as long-lived as many other trees, so use its delicate beauty to supplement more permanent trees in the garden.

Features: rounded or spreading, multi-stemmed, deciduous tree or shrub; red, purple, pink spring flowers; fall foliage **Height:** 20–30' **Spread:** 15–30' **Hardiness:** zones 4–9

River Birch

Betula

When it comes to showy bark, the river birch tree is unmatched. As it ages, its attractive, peeling bark adds a whole new dimension to the garden.

Growing

River birch grows well in **full sun, partial shade** or **light shade**. The soil should be of **average to high fertility, moist** and fairly **well drained**. Periodic flooding is tolerated but persistently wet soils will kill these trees.

Tips

Birch trees are often used as specimens. Their small leaves and open canopy provide light shade that allows perennials, annuals and lawns to flourish underneath. If you have enough space in your garden, birches look attractive when grown in groups near natural or artificial water features.

Recommended

B. nigra (river birch, black birch, red birch) has shaggy, cinnamon brown bark that flakes off in sheets when the tree is young, but the bark thickens and becomes more ridged as the tree matures. It grows 60–90' tall and spreads 40–60'. This species is resistant to pests and diseases. The cultivar **'Heritage'** is noted for its exceptional, peeling bark.

B. nigra 'Little King' (above), *B. nigra* (below)

The bark of certain species has been used to make canoes, shelters and utensils.

Features: open, deciduous tree; attractive foliage; bark; fall color; winter and spring catkins **Height:** 25–90' **Spread:** 15–60' **Hardiness:** zones 3–8

Rose-of-Sharon

Hibiscus

H. syriacus 'Woodbridge' (above), *H. syriacus* 'Red Heart' (below)

To create a tropical look in your backyard, search no further than Rose-of-Sharon.

Growing

Rose-of-Sharon prefers **full sun** but tolerates partial shade. It responds well in **fertile** soil that is **humus rich, moist** and **well drained**, but it tolerates poor soil and wet spots.

Pinch young shrubs to encourage bushy growth. Young plants can be trained to form a single-stemmed tree by selectively pruning out all but the strongest stem. The flowers form on the current year's growth; prune the tip growth in late winter or early spring for larger but fewer flowers.

Tips

Rose-of-Sharon is best used in shrub or mixed borders. This shrub develops unsightly bare branches towards its base as it matures. Plant low, bushy perennials or shrubs around the base to hide the bare stems. The leaves emerge late in spring and drop early in fall. Planting Rose-of-Sharon along with evergreen shrubs will make up for the short period of leafiness.

Recommended

H. syriacus is an erect, multi-stemmed shrub that bears dark pink flowers from mid-summer to fall. Many cultivars are available, including **'Blue Bird'** that bears large blue flowers with red centers, and the **Goddess Series**, bearing big, single, thick, long-lasting flowers in a variety of bright colors. **'Red Heart'** bears white flowers with dark red centers.

Features: bushy, upright, deciduous shrub; solid or bicolored mid-summer to fall flowers
Height: 8–12' **Spread:** 6–8'
Hardiness: zones 5–10

Snowbell

Styrax

Snowbells are easy to admire for their delicate, shapely appearance and dangling flowers that are clustered along the undersides of the branches.

Growing

Snowbells grow well in **full sun, partial shade** or **light shade**. The soil should be **fertile, humus rich, neutral to acidic, moist** and **well drained**. Snowbells perform poorly in alkaline soils.

Tips

Snowbells can be used to provide light shade in shrub or mixed borders. They can also be included in woodland gardens, and they make interesting specimens near entryways or patios.

Recommended

S. americana (American snowbell) is a rounded shrub

S. japonica (above & below)

that grows 6–9' tall and a little less wide. It produces zigzagging stems clothed in bright green foliage and fragrant, single or clusters of nodding, bell-shaped, white flowers in mid-summer.

S. japonica (Japanese snowbell) is a small, graceful, upright tree. It has arching branches from which white blossoms dangle in late spring. The species grows 25–30' tall and wide. **'Carillon'** is a weeping variety, and **'Emerald Pagoda'** displays a similar habit but at twice the size. **'Pink Chimes'** is slightly more upright in form with pink blossoms.

S. obassia (fragrant snowbell) is a broad, columnar tree that bears white flowers in long clusters at the branch ends in early summer.

Features: upright, rounded, spreading or columnar, deciduous tree or shrub; late-spring to early-summer flowers in pink or white; foliage **Height:** 6–30' **Spread:** 6–30' **Hardiness:** zones 4–8

Spirea
Spiraea

S. japonica 'Goldmound' (above), *S. x vanhouttei* (below)

Spireas, seen in so many gardens and with dozens of cultivars, remain undeniable favorites. With a wide range of forms, sizes and colors of both foliage and flowers, spireas have many possible uses in the landscape.

Growing

Spireas prefer **full sun**. To help prevent foliage burn, provide protection from very hot sun. The soil should be **fertile, acidic, moist** and **well drained**.

Tips

Spireas are used in shrub or mixed borders, in rock gardens and as informal screens and hedges.

Recommended

Many species, cultivars and hybrids of spirea are available, including **S. japonica**, an upright, shrubby species that grows 4–6' tall and bears 8" wide clusters of pink flowers atop the lush green foliage. **S. nipponica** 'Snowmound' is a compact, spreading shrub that grows only 2–3' tall and wide with a profusion of white flowers in late spring. **S. x vanhouttei** (bridal wreath spirea, Vanhoutte spirea) is a dense, bushy shrub with arching branches that bears clusters of white flowers. Check with your local nursery or garden center to see what is available.

Features: round, bushy, deciduous shrub; attractive summer flowers in white or pink
Height: 1–10' **Spread:** 1–12'
Hardiness: zones 3–9

Summersweet

Clethra

Summersweet attracts butter-flies and other pollinators and is one of the best shrubs for adding fragrance to your garden.

Growing

Summersweet grows best in **light** or **partial shade**. The soil should be **fertile, humus rich, acidic, moist** and **well drained**.

Tips

Although not aggressive, this shrub tends to sucker, forming a colony of stems. Use it in a border or in a woodland garden. The light shade along the edge of a woodland is also an ideal location.

Recommended

C. alnifolia is a large, rounded, upright, colony-forming shrub. It grows 3–8' tall, spreading 3–6', and bears attractive spikes of white flowers in mid- to late sum-mer. The foliage turns yellow in fall. Recommended cultivars include the medium-growing **'Anne Bidwell,'** which bears extra large clusters of late-season flow-ers, low-growing **'Hummingbird,'** and **'Ruby Spice,'** a selection with reddish pink flowers.

C. alnifolia 'Paniculata' (above & below)

Summersweet is useful in damp, shaded gardens, where the late-season flowers are much appreciated.

Features: attractive, rounded, suckering, deciduous shrub; fragrant, white or reddish pink summer flowers; colorful fall foliage
Height: 2–8' **Spread:** 3–8'
Hardiness: zones 3–9

Sweetspire
Itea

I. virginica (above & below)

A straggly shrub in the wild, sweetspire has been refined through the development of new cultivars and now offers neat, compact additions to the shrub border.

Growing

Sweetspire grows well in all light conditions from **full sun to full shade**, though plants grown in full sun develop the best fall color. The habit is more arching in sun and more upright in shade. The soil should be **fertile** and **moist**. Sweetspire is fairly adaptable.

One-third of the older growth can be removed to the ground each year once flowering ends. Do not prune in early spring or you will lose the current season's flower buds.

Tips

Sweetspire is an excellent shrub for low-lying and moist areas of the garden. It grows well near streams and water features. It is also a fine choice for plantings near decks, patios and pathways, where the scent of the fragrant flowers can be enjoyed.

Sweetspire can be used individually or in small groups in the home garden, and it can be planted in masses in larger areas.

Recommended

I. virginica (Virginia sweetspire) is an upright to arching, suckering shrub. Spikes of fragrant, white flowers appear in early summer, and the leaves turn shades of purple and red in fall. **'Henry's Garnet'** bears many long, white flower spikes and consistently develops dark red-purple fall color. LITTLE HENRY ('Sprich') is a compact cultivar with a low, mound-forming habit. It bears bright white flower spikes and develops bright red fall color.

Features: upright to arching, deciduous shrub; fragrant, white flowers; fall color
Height: 2–10' **Spread:** 3–10' or more
Hardiness: zones 5–9

Tulip Poplar
Liriodendron

This stately native tree has, as its common name suggests, tulip-like flowers of greenish yellow and orange and uniquely shaped leaves that are also reminiscent of tulip blossoms.

Growing

Tulip poplar grows well in **full sun** or **partial shade**. The soil should be **average to rich, slightly acidic** and **moist**. This tree needs plenty of room for its roots to grow. It does not tolerate drought. Little pruning is required.

Tips

This beautiful, massive tree needs a lot of room to grow. Parks, golf courses and large gardens can host this tree as a specimen or in a group planting, but its susceptibility to drought and need for root space make it a poor choice as a specimen, shade or street tree on smaller properties.

Recommended

L. tulipifera is native to the eastern U.S. It's known more for its unusual leaves than for its tulip-like flowers because the blooms are often borne high in the tree and go unnoticed until the falling petals litter the ground. The foliage turns golden yellow in fall. The fruit is a cone-shaped cluster of long-winged nutlets, green at first and maturing to pale brown. The species can grow to 75–100' tall with 30–50' spreads.

L. tulipifera (above & below)

The genus name Liriodendron *comes from the Greek and means 'lily tree.'*

Features: large, rounded, oval, deciduous tree; early-summer flowers; foliage; fruit
Height: 50–100' **Spread:** 20–50'
Hardiness: zones 4–9

Weigela
Weigela

Weigelas have been improved through breeding, and specimens with more compact forms, longer flowering periods and greater cold tolerance are now available.

Growing
Weigela prefers **full sun** but tolerates partial shade. The soil should be **fertile** and **well drained**. This plant adapts to most well-drained soil conditions.

Tips
Weigelas can be used in shrub or mixed borders, in open woodland gardens and as informal barrier plantings.

Recommended
W. florida is a spreading shrub with arching branches that bears clusters of dark pink flowers. Many hybrids and cultivars are available. Some of the best selections include MIDNIGHT WINE, a low-mounding dwarf with dark burgundy foliage; **'Red Prince,'** with dark red flowers; **'Rubidor,'** with yellow foliage and red flowers; **'Variegata,'** with yellow-green variegated foliage and pink flowers; and WINE AND ROSES, with dark burgundy foliage and rosy pink flowers.

W. florida 'Variegata' (above), *W. florida* cultivar (below)

Weigela is one of the longest-blooming shrubs, with the main flush of blooms lasting as long as six weeks. It often re-blooms if sheared lightly after the first flowers fade.

Features: upright or low, spreading, deciduous shrub; late-spring to early-summer flowers in shades of red, white, pink; foliage **Height:** 1–9' **Spread:** 1–12' **Hardiness:** zones 3–8

Bonica

Modern Shrub Rose

Bonica was the first modern shrub rose to be named an All-America Selection. The blooms have a light and sweet fragrance. Bright orange hips follow the double, pink flowers.

Growing

Bonica prefers **full sun** and **fertile, moist, well-drained** soil with at least **5% organic matter** mixed in. It can tolerate light breezes, but keep it out of strong winds. Roses are heavy feeders and drinkers and do not like to share their root space with other plants. This disease-resistant, hardy rose tolerates shade and poor soils.

Tips

Bonica suits just about any location. Rose growers recommend it for mixed beds, containers, hedges, cut-flower gardens or as a groundcover, standard or specimen.

Recommended

Rosa '**Bonica**' is a tidy, spreading rose of modest size that blooms profusely through most of the growing season. It bears an abundance of semi-glossy, rich green foliage that is beautiful enough to stand on its own.

This beautiful rose has maintained worldwide popularity since its introduction.

Also called: Bonica '82, Meidomonac, Demon, Bonica Meidiland **Features:** repeat blooming, medium pink summer to fall flowers; easy maintenance; colorful hips **Height:** 3–5' **Spread:** 3–4' **Hardiness:** zones 4–9

Carefree Beauty

Modern Shrub · Landscape Rose

This magnificent rose was developed by the late Dr. Griffith J. Buck at Iowa State University. It is one in the long line of his 'prairie' showstoppers that are perfectly suited to Virginia gardens.

Growing

Carefree Beauty requires a location in **full sun**. **Well-drained, organically rich, slightly acidic** soil is best, but this shrub rose tolerates light shade and poorer soils.

Tips

This upright shrub has a spreading habit, which makes it an ideal candidate for a low-maintenance hedge. It also makes a fine specimen and complements other flowering shrubs and perennials in mixed borders.

Recommended

Rosa **'Carefree Beauty'** bears small clusters of deep pink, 4 1/2" wide, semi-double blossoms, not once but twice throughout the growing season. The blossoms are large, which balances out the small quantities of flowers produced at the end of each stem. The fragrant flowers beautifully complement the smooth, olive green foliage. Orange-red hips follow after the flowers, adding winter interest to the landscape into the early months of spring.

Also called: Audace **Features:** fragrant, large, deep pink blossoms; disease-free foliage; vigorous growth habit **Height:** 5–6' **Spread:** 4–5' **Hardiness:** zones 3–9

Double Delight

Hybrid Tea Rose

Double Delight is aptly named: it delights with its strong, sweet, lightly spicy fragrance and its unique flower color. The fully double, high-centered flowers open cream with red edges and gradually darken to solid red. Heat intensifies the color.

Growing

Double Delight prefers **full sun** and **fertile, moist, well-drained** soil with at least **5% organic matter** mixed in. It can tolerate light breezes, but keep it out of strong winds. This rose requires supplemental fertilizer and a lot of moisture, and does not like to share root space with other plants.

Blackspot can be a problem for Double Delight. Cool, wet weather can promote mildew.

Tips

It's difficult to find a place for this unique flower color in a bed or border. Try planting it in a warm, dry location or in a container where it can be easily monitored for disease.

Recommended

Rosa **'Double Delight'** is an upright, irregularly branched plant with mid-green foliage. Its fragrance is unaffected by temperature, light or age.

Double Delight is a long-lasting cut flower and a good choice for competition and exhibition.

Also called: Andeli **Features:** repeat blooming; cream with carmine-edged, summer-to-fall flowers; fragrance **Height:** 3–4' **Spread:** 24–36"
Hardiness: zones 6–9

Dublin Bay
Rambling · Climbing Rose

Dublin Bay is one of the best red-blooming ramblers/climbers available. It blooms longer and more frequently than just about any other climber.

Growing
Dublin Bay prefers **full sun** and **moist, well-drained** soil. It holds up well in extreme heat but should not be planted in a windy location.

Tips
This rambler/climber fans out well on low fences and trellises. It is attractive climbing up obelisks, pillars, pergolas or arches. It can also be pruned into an informal hedge.

Recommended
Rosa **'Dublin Bay'** is a tall, flowering shrub that grows 8–14' tall. It has a reliable growth habit and weatherproof flowers. It requires little maintenance and is highly resistant to disease. The large, oval buds open to well-shaped, double blooms. The moderately thorny stems support dark green, shiny foliage.

The first flush of blooms can last up to six weeks or more.

Features: bright red flowers; repeat blooming habit; disease resistance **Height:** 8–14'
Spread: 5–7'; dependent on support
Hardiness: zones 4–11

Hot Tamale

Miniature Rose

*H*ot Tamale is a little flower factory, producing wave after wave of blooms that transform from one color to another.

Growing

This beautiful miniature rose thrives in **full sun,** and **moist** but **well-drained, fertile** soil.

Tips

Miniature roses are often planted in containers to focus on their smaller stature and to make sure they're not lost in a large bed of mixed annuals, perennials and shrubs. With its bright colors, Hot Tamale is a great choice for containers on porches or patios.

Recommended

Rosa '**Hot Tamale**' produces tiny, 1 1/2–2" wide, lightly scented blossoms. When they first emerge, the flowers are a striking yellow-orange blend. Over time, a vibrant pink slightly obscures the yellow coloring until finally the three colors merge, resulting in an electric glow unlike any other rose color. It has a bushy and compact form. The stout canes are covered with dense, healthy foliage and few prickles. The flower color lasts and lasts against the dark, semi-glossy foliage.

Hot Tamale was bred by Dr. Keith W. Zary of the U.S. in 1993. The year following its introduction, it won the American Rose Society Award of Excellence for miniature roses, an honor reserved for the best.

Also called: Sunbird **Features:** colorful, bicolored flowers; tiny form and habit
Height: 18–22" **Spread:** 24–28"
Hardiness: zones 5–11

Iceberg
Floribunda Rose

Over 40 years have passed since this exceptional rose was first introduced, and its continued popularity proves it can stand the test of time.

Growing
Iceberg grows best in **full sun**. The soil should be **fertile, humus rich, slightly acidic, moist** and **well drained**. Winter protection is required. Deadhead to prolong blooming.

Tips
Iceberg is a popular addition to mixed borders and beds, and also works well as a specimen. Plant it in a well-used area or near a window where its flower fragrance can best be enjoyed. This rose can also be included in large planters or patio containers.

Recommended
Rosa 'Iceberg' is a vigorous shrub with a rounded, bushy habit and light green foliage. It produces clusters of semi-double flowers in several flushes from early summer to fall. A climbing variation of this rose is reputed to be the best climbing white rose ever developed.

Also called: fée des neiges
Features: bushy habit; strong, sweet fragrance; white early-summer to fall flowers, sometimes flushed with pink during cool or wet weather **Height:** 3–4' **Spread:** 3–4'
Hardiness: zones 5–8

Knockout

Modern Shrub · Landscape Rose

*T*his rose is simply one of the best new shrub roses to hit the market in years.

Growing

Knockout grows best in **full sun**. The soil should be **fertile, humus rich, slightly acidic, moist** and **well drained**. This rose blooms most prolifically in warm weather but has deeper red flowers in cooler weather. Deadhead lightly to keep the plant tidy and to encourage blooming.

Tips

This vigorous rose makes a good addition to a mixed bed or border, and it is attractive when planted in groups of three or more. It can be mass planted to create a large display or grown singly as an equally beautiful specimen.

Recommended

Rosa 'Knockout' has a lovely, rounded form with glossy, green leaves that turn to shades of burgundy in fall. The bright, cherry red flowers are borne in clusters of 3–15 almost all summer and into fall. Orange-red hips last well into winter. **'Double Knockout,' 'Pink Knockout'** and a light pink selection called **'Blushing Knockout'** are all available. All have excellent disease resistance.

If you've been afraid that roses need too much care, you'll appreciate the hardiness and disease resistance of this low-maintenance beauty.

Features: rounded habit; light, tea-rose-scented, mid-summer to fall flowers in shades of pink or red; disease resistance **Height:** 3–4' **Spread:** 3–4' **Hardiness:** zones 4–10

New Dawn
Climbing Rose

*I*ntroduced in 1930, New Dawn is still a favorite climbing rose of gardeners and rosarians.

New Dawn was inducted into the World Federation of Rose Societies' Hall of Fame in 1997.

Growing
New Dawn grows best in **full sun**. The soil should be **average to fertile, humus rich, slightly acidic, moist** and **well drained**. This rose is disease resistant.

Tips
Train New Dawn to climb pergolas, walls, pillars, arbors, trellises and fences. With some judicious pruning it can be trained to form a bushy shrub or hedge. Plant this rose where the summer-long profusion of blooms will welcome visitors to your home.

Recommended
Rosa 'New Dawn' is a vigorous climber with upright arching canes and glossy green foliage. It bears pale pink flowers, singly or in small clusters.

Features: glossy green foliage; climbing habit; long blooming period; pale pearl pink flowers; sweet, apple-like fragrance **Height:** 10–15'
Spread: 10–15' **Hardiness:** zones 4–9

Pat Austin

English (Austin) Rose

Pat Austin introduced a new and vivid color combination: rich copper shades on the uppersides of the petals and pale amber yellow on the undersides. It is difficult to miss this exceptional contrast as the fragrant flowers open and expand.

Growing

Pat Austin prefers **full sun** and **fertile, moist, well-drained** soil with at least **5% organic matter** mixed in. Keep it out of strong winds.

Tips

Pat Austin blends beautifully into mixed shrub borders, informal beds or containers. It can also be trained as a short climber.

Recommended

Rosa **'Pat Austin'** is a vigorous, medium-sized, gracefully spreading plant. The semi-glossy, deep green foliage complements the large, open, deeply-cupped, coppery flowers. The flowers have a sharp, fruity fragrance.

Pat Austin may be difficult to find because it is such a recent introduction, but it is well worth the search.

Features: repeat blooming; coppery amber, yellow summer to fall flowers; graceful form
Height: 3' **Spread:** 4'
Hardiness: zones 5–9

Queen Elizabeth
Grandiflora Rose

The grandiflora classification was originally created to accommodate this rose. Queen Elizabeth is one of the most widely grown and best-loved roses.

Growing
Queen Elizabeth grows best in **full sun**. The soil should be **average to fertile, humus rich, slightly acidic, moist** and **well drained**, but this durable rose adapts to most soils and tolerates high heat and humidity. Prune plants back to 5–7 canes and 5–7 buds each spring.

Tips
Queen Elizabeth is a trouble-free rose that makes a good addition to mixed borders and beds. It can also be used as a specimen, to form a hedge or grown in a large planter. Its flowers are borne on sturdy stems that make them useful for floral arrangements.

Recommended
Rosa **'Queen Elizabeth'** is a bushy shrub with glossy, dark green foliage and dark stems. The pink, cup-shaped, double flowers may be borne singly or in clusters of several flowers.

Queen Elizabeth has won many honors and was named World's Favorite Rose in 1979 by the World Federation of Rose Societies.

Features: glossy, dark green, disease-resistant foliage; soft, lightly scented, pearly pink summer to fall flowers **Height:** 4–6'
Spread: 30–36" **Hardiness:** zones 5–9

American Bittersweet

Celastrus

C. scandens (above & below)

American bittersweet is a rough-and-tumble, low-maintenance, woody climber that lends a wild look to your garden. Highly decorative clusters of fruit burst forth in fall.

Growing

American bittersweet grows well in **full sun** but tolerates partial shade. It prefers **poor soil** but adapts to almost any well-drained soil.

Male and female flowers usually bloom on separate plants. Both sexes, planted in close proximity, are needed for fruit production. American bittersweet is often sold with a male and a female plant in one pot. Water them well.

Tips

American bittersweet belongs at the edge of a woodland garden and in a natural-ized area. It quickly covers fences, arbors, trellises, posts and walls. As a groundcover it can mask rubble and tree stumps, and effectively controls erosion on hard-to-maintain slopes. All parts of American bittersweet are said to be poisonous.

This vine can damage or kill young trees or shrubs if it is allowed to twine around the stems.

Recommended

C. scandens (American bittersweet, staff vine) is a vigorous, twining vine with dark green, glossy foliage that turns bright yellow in fall. Small, yellow-green to whitish flowers bloom in late spring followed by showy fruit. '**Indian Brave**' and '**Indian Maid**,' the male and female cultivar pair, are hardier than the species.

Features: fast growth; twining stems; fruit; fall color **Height:** 6 1/2–10' **Spread:** 3–6'
Hardiness: zones 3–8

Carolina Jessamine
Gelsemium

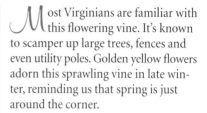

Most Virginians are familiar with this flowering vine. It's known to scamper up large trees, fences and even utility poles. Golden yellow flowers adorn this sprawling vine in late winter, reminding us that spring is just around the corner.

Growing
Carolina jessamine thrives in locations with **full sun**. It will grow in partial shade but produces fewer flowers. The soil should be **moist**, **well drained** and **fertile**.

Pinch the new growth back to encourage a more dense growth habit. Cut it back to approximately 2–3' high when the growth is thin at the bottom and the top is falling over because of the weight.

Tips
This vine can be grown on a decorative trellis, pergola, or an arbor. It is often used to adorn mailboxes and just about anything that requires a bit of color and a vertical element.

All parts of this plant are poisonous.

Recommended
G. sempervirens is a vigorous vine that produces twining stems without the aid of tendrils. Masses of fragrant, funnel-shaped flowers are borne in late winter in shades of golden to pale yellow. Dark, glossy foliage on rich brown stems is the perfect complement to the brightly colored blossoms.

G. sempervirens (above & below)

This vine can also be used as an effective groundcover when maintained. It is best to plant it in a place where it can be left to roam and won't be bothered once established.

Features: bright yellow flower clusters; lush foliage; habit **Height:** 15–20' **Spread:** 4–5' **Hardiness:** zones 7–9

Clematis
Clematis

There are so many species, hybrids and cultivars of clematis that it is possible to have one in bloom all season.

Growing

Clematis plants prefer **full sun** but tolerate partial shade. The soil should be **fertile, humus rich, moist** and **well drained**. These vines enjoy warm, sunny weather, but the roots prefer to be cool. A thick layer of mulch or planting of low, shade-providing perennials will protect the tender roots. The rootball of vining clematis should be planted about 2" beneath the surface of the soil. Clematis are quite cold hardy but fare best when protected from winter wind.

Tips

Clematis vines can climb up structures such as trellises, railings, fences and arbors. They can also be allowed to grow over shrubs and up trees and can be used as groundcover.

Recommended

There are many species, hybrids and cultivars of clematis. The flower forms, blooming times and sizes of the plants can vary. Clematis comes in just about every form and color imaginable. Check with your local garden center to see what is available.

Features: twining habit; blue, purple, pink, yellow, red, white early to late-summer flowers; decorative seedheads **Height:** 10–17' or more **Spread:** 5' or more **Hardiness:** zones 3–8

C. 'Jackmanii Rubra' (above), *C.* 'Gravetye Beauty' (below)

Plant two clematis varieties that bloom at the same time to provide a mix of color and texture.

Climbing Hydrangea
Hydrangea

H. anomala subsp. petiolaris (above & below)

Growing
Climbing hydrangea grows best in **part shade** in **humus-rich, moist, well-drained, acidic** soil of **average fertility**. It adapts to full sun and to most soils as long as the soil remains moist. It appreciates shelter from the hot sun and from strong or drying winds.

Once established, prune out overly aggressive growth.

Tips
Climbing hydrangea is used as a climbing vine and also as a groundcover. It clings to structures by use of aerial roots and tends to stay flat when grown on flat surfaces such as walls. It will slowly cover walls and arbors, and anything that is nearby.

Recommended
H. anomala* subsp. *petiolaris is a vigorous, woody climber. The stems 'cling' by aerial roots or holdfasts. The foliage is reminiscent of other hydrangea species and the flower clusters are very similar in appearance to *H. macrophylla*, bearing flattened clusters of insignificant, fertile flowers, surrounded by open, infertile flowers in creamy white.

Climbing hydrangea is an attractive, pest-free vine that is great to use for growing up through a tree. The tree provides a structure to climb, and the tree's foliage helps shade the vine.

Features: attractive foliage; white summer flowers; habit **Height:** 60–80' or more when climbing; shrubby and sprawling without support **Spread:** dependent on support **Hardiness:** zones 5–9

Cross Vine

Bignonia

This native vine is known to grow very large and at a rapid rate. It blooms like crazy and will disguise ugly surfaces and structures in no time flat.

Growing

Cross vine tolerates a wide range of soil conditions but prefers **organically rich, well-drained** soil in **full sun**. Partial sun is tolerated but cross vine may flower less.

Prune after flowering and to train it on a support.

Tips

This twining plant will climb up just about anything. The stems climb by little suction-cup-like bits at the end of their tendrils and by rootlets called holdfast disks. When first planted, cross vine will need to be attached to the surface or structure it is to climb. Any type of garden structure can be used, along with stone or brick walls, fences, poles and trees.

Recommended

B. capreolata is a twining, vigorous vine that produces lush green foliage on its long, tough stems. Orange-yellow, tubular flowers with reddish throats emerge in spring and early summer. The foliage takes on a purplish red coloration as the days grow cooler in winter. Cultivars are available in other fiery colors as well.

B. capreolata 'Jeckyll' (above & below)

Cross vine is sometimes confused with trumpet creeper. Although they look somewhat similar, cross vine doesn't have the same invasive nature and blooms at a different time in the growing season.

Features: bright, fiery-colored flowers; vigorous twining habit **Height:** 30–50'
Spread: 20–40' **Hardiness:** zones 6–9

Honeysuckle
Lonicera

L. sempervirens (above)
L. x brownii 'Dropmore Scarlet' (below)

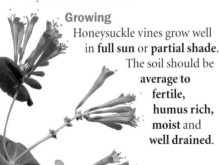

Honeysuckle vines can be rampant twining vines, but with careful placement, they won't overrun your garden. The fragrance of the flowers makes any effort worthwhile.

Growing

Honeysuckle vines grow well in **full sun** or **partial shade**. The soil should be **average to fertile, humus rich, moist** and **well drained**.

Tips

Honeysuckle vines can be trained to grow up a trellis, fence, arbor or other structure. In a large container near a porch it will ramble over the edges of the pot and up the railings with reckless abandon.

Recommended

L. japonica (Japanese honeysuckle) is a vigorous, woody climber with deeply-lobed leaves and tubular, fragrant, white flowers with a touch of purple. The flowers eventually change to a pale shade of yellow or cream, followed by blue-black berries. This species can grow up to 30' in height. Many cultivars and varieties are available with variegated foliage and colorful flowers.

L. periclymenum (woodbine honeysuckle) is a deciduous vine that grows 10–20' tall. It is very similar to *L. japonica* in appearance but is less aggressive. It bears fragrant, white to yellow flowers with a hint of red in summer and fall. Cultivars are available with flowers of varied color combinations, including 'Harlequin,' which bears pink flowers with creamy yellow throats.

L. sempervirens (trumpet honeysuckle, coral honeysuckle) bears orange or red flowers in late spring and early summer. Many cultivars and hybrids are available with flowers in yellow, red or scarlet, including *L. x brownii* 'Dropmore Scarlet,' one of the hardiest of the climbing honeysuckles, cold hardy to zone 4. It bears bright red flowers for most of summer.

Features: creamy white, yellow, orange, red, pink, scarlet late-spring and early-summer flowers; twining habit; fruit **Height:** 6–30' **Spread:** 6–20' **Hardiness:** zones 5–9

Virginia Creeper

Parthenocissus

P. quinquefolia (above & below)

Let a Virginia creeper embellish any garden that needs a look of wild abandon. Every fall, Virginia creeper explodes in a wildfire of color.

Growing
These vines grow well in any light from **full sun to full shade**. The soil should be **fertile** and **well drained**. The plants adapt to clay or sandy soils.

Tips
Virginia creeper does not require support because it has clinging rootlets that can adhere to just about any surface, even smooth wood, vinyl or metal. Give this plant a lot of space and let it cover a wall, fence or arbor. Virginia creeper can also be used as a groundcover.

Recommended
P. quinquefolia (Virginia creeper, woodbine) has dark green foliage. Each leaf, divided into five leaflets, turns flame red in fall.

Virginia creeper can cover the sides of buildings and help keep them cool in the summer heat. Cut the plants back to keep windows and doors accessible.

Features: summer and fall foliage; clinging habit **Height & Spread:** possibly 30–50', but limited by the size of support
Hardiness: zones 3–8

Wisteria
Wisteria

W. floribunda (left), *W. sinensis* (right)

oose clusters of purple hang like lace from the branches of wisteria. With prudent pruning, a gardener can create beautiful tree forms and attractive arbor specimens.

Growing
Wisterias grow well in **full sun** or **partial shade**. The soil should be of **average fertility, moist** and **well drained**. Too fertile a soil will produce a lot of vegetative growth but very few flowers. Avoid planting wisterias near a lawn where fertilizer may leach over to the vine.

Tips
These vines require something to twine around, such as an arbor or other sturdy structure. Select a permanent site; wisterias don't like being moved. They may send up suckers and can root wherever branches touch the ground.

All parts of these plants are poisonous.

Recommended
W. floribunda (Japanese wisteria) bears long, pendulous clusters of fragrant, blue, purple, pink or white flowers in late spring before the leaves emerge. Long, bean-like pods follow.

W. sinensis (Chinese wisteria) bears long, pendent clusters of fragrant, blue-purple flowers in late spring. **'Alba'** has white flowers.

To keep wisteria blooming sporadically all summer, prune off flowering spikes as soon as the flowers fade. A long-handled pole pruner works well. Wisteria sends out new blooming shoots until frost.

Features: blue, purple, pink, white flowers; foliage; twining habit **Height:** 20–50' or more **Spread:** 20–50' or more **Hardiness:** zones 4–8

Amaryllis
Hippeastrum

*A*maryllis is becoming quite the contender in the world of bulbs. More and more southern gardeners are indulging themselves in this showy, impressive bloomer.

Growing

Amaryllis prefers to grow in **full sun to light, dappled shade**. The soil should be **fertile** and **well drained**.

When planting, ensure that the top quarter of the bulb is above the soil surface. Remove the flower stem once the flowers are spent. Amaryllis isn't fond of being disturbed once established, but you can propagate this bulb by gently removing clumps of offsets from the mother bulb and planting them in another location.

Outside of zones 8–11, dig up the bulbs in fall, store them in dry cool place, and replant them in spring.

Tips

Amaryllis is well suited to mixed beds and borders when planted in clumps. It provides color in early spring; plant it where color is lacking during this period. It is also quite easy to grow in containers, giving a blast of color to your patio or balcony.

Recommended

Hippeastrum **hybrids** are available in abundance but in different subgroups. **Large Flowered hybrids** are bulbous perennials with flowers that grow to 4–6" in width. Many selections are available in a wide array of solid or bicolored combinations. **Miniature Flowered hybrids**

H. Large Flowered hybrids (above & below)

are equally showy but produce smaller-sized flowers in 3–4" diameters. This group also has a vast selection of colors and patterns that are sure to please.

Features: colorful flowers; habit
Height: 12–24" Spread: 6–8"
Hardiness: zones 9–11

Caladium

Caladium

C. x *hortulanum* hybrid (above)
C. x *hortulanum* 'Sweetheart' (below)

The mid-ribs and veining of caladium's striking foliage only strengthen the design, helping draw the eye to the smashing leaf colors. If you are searching for bold texture in the garden, caladiums are a must.

Growing

Caladiums prefer to grow in **partial to full shade** in **moist, well-drained, humus-rich, slightly acidic** soil.

Caladiums are tuberous plants that can be grown from seed or from tubers. Start growing tubers inside in a soil-less planting mix with soil temperature of at least 70° F. Once they have leafed-out they can handle soil temperatures down to 55° F. When planting out, add a little bonemeal or fishmeal to the planting hole. Make sure the knobby side of the tuber is facing up and is level with the soil surface or just under it.

Tips

Caladiums are excellent at providing a tropical feel to your garden. They do very well around water features and in woodland gardens. They are equally effective in the herbaceous border in mass or as specimens and are wonderful plants for containers. When grown in containers there is no need to dig the tubers in fall. Simply bring the whole container inside for the winter.

All parts of caladium may irritate the skin, and ingesting this plant will cause stomach upset.

Recommended

C. x *hortulanum* (*C. bicolor*) is native to the edge of woodlands in tropical South America. The often tufted, arrow-shaped foliage is dark green and variously marked and patterned with red, white, pink, green, rose, salmon, silver or bronze. Each leaf is 6–12" long.

Also called: elephant's ears, heart-of-Jesus, mother-in-law plant, angel wings
Features: ornate, patterned and colorful foliage; habit **Height:** 18–24" **Spread:** 18–24" **Hardiness:** treat as an annual

Calla Lily
Zantedeschia

This beautiful, exotic-looking plant was only available as a cut flower in the past. The introduction of new cultivars, however, has made it more readily available and worth planting.

Growing
Calla lilies grow best in **full sun**. The soil should be **fertile**, **humus rich** and **moist**. Callas grown in containers can be brought indoors for winter. Reduce watering in winter, keeping the soil just moist.

Tips
Calla lilies are ideal additions to mixed beds and borders, and work well as container specimens. Calla lilies are also a great addition to the water garden, as they will grow and thrive in wet locations and can even be partially submerged in shallow water.

Rather than moving large, cumbersome plants, it is sometimes easier to remove small divisions in fall and transfer them indoors over the winter.

Recommended
Z. aethiopica (white arum lily, white calla) forms a clump of arrow-shaped, glossy green leaves. It bears white flowers from late spring to midsummer. Several cultivars are available.

Z. elliottiana (yellow calla, golden calla) forms a basal clump of white-spotted, dark green, heart-shaped leaves. It grows 24–36" tall and spreads 8–12". This species bears yellow flowers in summer and is a parent plant of many popular hybrids.

Z. aethiopica 'Little Gem' (above)
Z. elliottiana 'Flame' (below)

Although they grow quite large, calla lilies can be grown as houseplants year-round but benefit from spending summer outdoors.

Features: white, yellow flowers; foliage
Height: 16–36" **Spread:** 8–24"
Hardiness: treat as an annual

Daffodil

Narcissus

Many gardeners automatically think of large, yellow, trumpet-shaped flowers when they think of daffodils, but there is a lot of variety in color, form and size among the daffodils.

Growing

Daffodils grow best in **full sun or light, dappled shade**. The soil should be **average to fertile, moist** and **well**

The cup in the center of a daffodil is called the corona, and the group of petals that surrounds the corona is called the perianth.

drained. Bulbs should be planted in fall, 2–8" deep, depending on the size of the bulb. The bigger the bulb, the deeper it should be planted. A rule of thumb is to measure the bulb from top to bottom and then multiply that number by three to know how deeply to plant.

Tips

Daffodils are often planted where they can be left to naturalize, in the light shade beneath a tree or in a woodland garden. In mixed beds and borders, the faded leaves are hidden by the summer foliage of other plants.

Recommended

Many species, hybrids and cultivars of daffodils are available. Flowers range from 1 1/2–6" across and can be solitary or borne in clusters. There are about 12 flower-form categories.

Features: white, yellow, peach, orange, pink, bicolored spring flowers **Height:** 4–24" **Spread:** 4–12" **Hardiness:** zones 3–9

Dahlia

Dahlia

The variation in size, shape and color of dahlia flowers is astonishing. You are sure to find at least one of these old-fashioned but popular plants that appeals to you.

Growing

Dahlias prefer **full sun**. The soil should be **fertile,** rich in **organic matter, moist** and **well drained**. All dahlias are tender, tuberous perennials treated as annuals. Tubers can be purchased and started early indoors. The tubers can also be lifted in fall and stored over winter in slightly moist peat moss. Pot them and keep them in a bright room after they start sprouting in mid- to late winter. Deadhead to keep plants tidy and blooming.

Tips

Dahlias make attractive, colorful additions to a mixed border. The smaller varieties make good edging plants and the larger ones make good alternatives to shrubs. Varieties with unusual or interesting flowers are attractive specimen plants.

Recommended

Of the many dahlia hybrids, most are grown from tubers but a few can be started from seed. Many hybrids are classified and sold based on flower shape, such as collarette, decorative or peony-flowered. The flowers range in size from 2–12" and are available in many shades. The foliage is decorative too, ranging in color from bright

Dahlia hybrids in cutting bed (above)

green to bronze to purple. Check with your local garden center to see what is available.

Features: summer to fall flowers in shades of purple, pink, white, yellow, orange, red; some bicolored, attractive foliage; bushy habit
Height: 8"–5' Spread: 8–18"
Hardiness: tender perennial; treat as an annual

Gladiolus

Gladiolus

Grandiflorus hybrid (above), 'Homecoming' (below)

Plant corms in spring, 4–6" deep, once soil has warmed. Corms can also be started early indoors. Plant a few corms each week for about a month to prolong the blooming period.

Tips

Planted in groups in beds and borders, glads make a bold statement. Corms can also be pulled up in fall and stored in damp peat moss in a cool, frost-free location for the winter.

Perhaps best known as a cut flower, gladiolas (glads) add an air of extravagance to the garden.

Growing

Glads grow best in **full sun** but tolerate partial shade. The soil should be **fertile, humus rich, moist** and **well drained**. Flower spikes may need staking and a sheltered location out of the wind to prevent them from blowing over.

Recommended

Gladiolus **hybrids** have flowers that come in almost every imaginable shade, except blue. Plants are commonly grouped in three classifications: **Grandiflorus** is the best known, each corm producing a single spike of large, often ruffled flowers; **Nanus**, the hardiest group, survives in zone 3 with protection and produces several spikes of up to 7 flowers; and **Primulinus** produces a single spike of up to 23 flowers which grow farther apart than those of the grandiflorus.

Over 10,000 hybrid cultivars of Gladiolus *have been developed.*

Features: brightly colored, mid- to late-summer flowers in almost every color except blue
Height: 18"–6' **Spread:** 6–12"
Hardiness: zone 8; treat as an annual

Iris

Iris

Irises are steeped in history and lore. Many say the flower color range of bearded irises approximates that of a rainbow.

Growing

Irises prefer **full sun** but tolerate very light or dappled shade. The soil should be of **average fertility** and **well drained**. Japanese iris and Siberian iris prefer a moist but well-drained soil.

Divide in late summer or early autumn. When dividing bearded iris rhizomes, replant with the flat side of the foliage fan facing the garden. Dust the toe-shaped rhizome with a powder cleanser before planting to help prevent soft rot. Deadhead irises to keep them tidy.

Tips

All irises are popular border plants, but crested iris and yellow flag iris are also useful alongside streams or ponds. Dwarf cultivars make attractive additions to rock gardens.

Wash your hands after handling irises because they can cause severe internal irritation if ingested. You may not want to plant them close to places where children play.

Recommended

There are many iris species and hybrids available. Among the most popular is the bearded iris, often a hybrid of **I. germanica**. It has the widest range of flower colors. **I. cristata**

I. pseudoacorus (above)
I. germanica 'Stepping Out' (below)

(crested iris) is a low-growing species that bears multi-colored blossoms and is native to the south. **I. pseudoacorus** (yellow flag iris) is a water dweller and tolerates those wet locations where little else thrives. Check with your local garden center to find out what's available.

Features: spring, summer and sometimes fall flowers in almost every color combination, including bicolored and multi-colored; attractive foliage **Height:** 4–48" **Spread:** 6–48" **Hardiness:** zones 3–10

Lily
Lilium

Asiatic hybrids (above), 'Stargazer' (below)

Decorative clusters of large, richly colored blooms grace these tall plants. Flowers are produced at different times of the season, depending on the hybrid, and it is possible to have lilies blooming all season if a variety of cultivars are chosen.

Growing

Lilies grow best in **full sun** but like to have their **roots shaded**. The soil should be rich in **organic matter, fertile, moist** and **well drained**.

Tips

Lilies are often grouped in beds and borders and can be naturalized in woodland gardens and near water features. These plants are narrow but tall; plant at least three plants together to create some volume.

Recommended

The many species, hybrids and cultivars available are grouped by type. Visit your local garden center to see what is available. The following are two popular groups of lilies. **Asiatic hybrids** bear clusters of flowers in early summer or mid-summer and are available in a wide range of colors. **Oriental hybrids** bear clusters of large, fragrant, white, pink or red flowers in mid- and late summer.

Lily bulbs should be planted in fall before the first frost but can also be planted in spring if bulbs are available.

Features: early-, mid- or late-season flowers in shades of orange, yellow, peach, pink, purple, red, white **Height:** 24–60" **Spread:** 12" **Hardiness:** zones 4–8

Spring Star Flower

Ipheion

I. uniflorum 'Alba' (left), *I. uniflorum* 'Wisley Blue' (right)

What's more representative of a new spring season than a blooming, bulbous perennial with wildflower appeal? Spring star flower is unique and deserves wider use throughout the South.

Growing

Spring star flower grows well in **full sun to partial shade**. The soil should be **humus rich, fertile** and **well drained** but moist.

Tips

Spring star flower is ideal for rock gardens, mixed beds, borders and as an underplanting to larger-growing perennials, including hostas, peonies and daylilies. As the perennials emerge and mature, the flowering and foliage of spring star flower begins to die back for the season. It is also useful for naturalizing among grasses and woodlands.

Recommended

I. uniflorum is a vigorous, clump-forming perennial that emerges from a bulbous root. It produces narrow, strap-like foliage and single flowers with overlapping petals. Often the flowers are a pale silvery blue. The scented flowers are borne in other colors, including white, deep violet or lilac-blue. Many cultivars are available at your local garden center.

Features: starry-shaped, fragrant, colorful flowers in pale silvery blue, white, deep violet, lilac-blue; habit **Height:** 6–8" **Spread:** 4–6" **Hardiness:** zones 6–9

The bulbs should be planted approximately 2" deep and apart. Fall is the best time to plant, and division is unnecessary. The bulbs become more attractive as they multiply into larger clumps.

Summer Snowflake

Leucojum

L. aestivum 'Gravetye Giant' (left), *L. aestivum* (right)

Summer snowflake is one of the easiest bulbs to grow in the South, giving huge returns for little effort.

Growing

Summer snowflake grows well in areas with **full to partial sun** but not direct sun. The soil should be **moist, humus rich** and **very well drained**.

Tips

This flowering bulb is always attractive in rock gardens. It can be used for naturalizing and planting in understories

Summer snowflake is well known throughout the South and has been shared with family and friends from one generation to the next.

with adequate light. It will also pack a punch when planted in large groups or en masse in mixed beds and borders.

Recommended

L. aestivum produces strap- or grass-like leaves in an upright clump. Nodding, bell-shaped, white flowers dotted with green along the flower tips sit atop tall stems. The flowers emit a chocolate-like scent. The species grows approximately 1–1 1/2' tall with or without the flowers. **'Gravetye Giant'** grows taller than the species and produces larger flowers.

Features: nodding, fragrant, white flowers; habit **Height:** 12–18" **Spread:** 10–12" **Hardiness:** zones 4–9

Tulip

Tulipa

Tulips, with their beautifully colored flowers, are a welcome sight in the first warm days of spring.

Growing

Tulips grow best in **full sun**. The flowers tend to bend toward the light in light or partial shade. The soil should be **fertile** and **well drained**. Plant bulbs in fall. Cold-treated bulbs can be planted in spring. Although tulips can repeat bloom, many hybrids perform best if planted new each year. Species and older cultivars are the best choice for naturalizing.

Tips

Tulips provide the best display when mass planted in flowerbeds and borders. They can also be grown in containers and can be forced to bloom early in indoor pots. Some species and older cultivars can be naturalized in meadow and wildflower gardens.

Recommended

There are about 100 species of tulips and thousands of hybrids and cultivars. They are generally divided into 15 groups based on bloom time and flower appearance. Tulips come in dozens of shades, with many bicolored and multi-colored varieties. Blue is the only color not available. Purchase your tulips in early fall for the best selection.

When choosing tulip bulbs, remember that the bigger the bulb, the bigger the bloom.

Features: spring flowers in all colors except blue **Height:** 6–30" **Spread:** 2–8" **Hardiness:** zones 3–8; often grown as an annual

Wood Sorrel
Oxalis

O. crassipes (left), *O. crassipes* 'Alba' (right)

Some may associate this clover-like bulbous perennial with the weed, but this group of plants has so much to offer, and wants little in return.

Growing

Wood sorrel prefers **full to partial sun** in locations with **humus-rich, fertile, moist** but **well-drained** soil.

Tips

Wood sorrel is a pretty little ground-cover in smaller areas, including the gaps between stepping stones, the understories of larger perennials and shrubs, and along woodlands and pathways. It is often planted in rock gardens, hypertufa containers and gravelly alpine settings.

Recommended

O. crassipes (wood sorrel, pink wood sorrel) often blooms in early summer and again in fall. This species grows 4–10" tall. It is tolerant of drought but prefers moist shade. Cultivars are available, including **'Alba,'** which bears white flowers and is happy in sun or light shade, though a little shelter is preferred in extremely hot zones. **'Light Pink'** bears pale pink blossoms.

The family is Oxalidaceae and the name is derived from the Greek word 'oxys,' which means sharp, and 'als,' the word for salt. The name refers to the acid taste of the sap.

Features: interesting foliage; uses; habit; colorful, white, pale pink flowers Height: 4–10" Spread: 4–10" Hardiness: zones 5–9

Chamomile
Chamaemelum

C. *nobile* 'German' (left & right)

You too can grow your own crop of medicinal chamomile for those moments when you need to slow down and calm your frazzled nerves.

Growing

Chamomile prefers to grow in locations with **full sun to light shade. Well-drained, moist** and **light** soil is best.

Tips

This aromatic herb is perfectly suited to medicinal herb gardens. Chamomile is also an attractive plant and mixes well into borders but it can spread, becoming invasive. It is often used as a ground-cover between stepping stones and is well suited to cottage garden settings and container culture.

Features: aromatic foliage; daisy-like, white, yellow flowers **Height:** 3–12" **Spread:** 12" **Hardiness:** zones 6–9

Recommended

C. nobile 'German' is a mat-forming, stalkless plant with fragrant, divided foliage. It bears daisy-like flowers in summer. Cultivars with double flowers and a non-flowering selections are available.

The flowers should be harvested when they are fully open. Once dried, the flowers can be used to make a tea that's often used as a sedative. This herb has also been used in cosmetics and crafts for generations.

Chervil
Anthriscus

A. cerefolium

Chervil has earned its rightful place in the kitchen. It's been used for centuries by cooks for various culinary purposes, and by homeopaths for medicinal purposes, but it is also grown by gardeners for its delicate beauty.

Growing
Chervil grows well in **partial shade** or **full sun**, in any **well-drained** soil.

Chervil goes to seed very quickly in locations with hot summers, including the South in general. To prevent this from occurring, pinch the flowers out as they begin to emerge, allowing the plant to divert its energy into dense, leafy growth. Chervil can also be seeded in fall or winter because of its preference for cooler weather.

Tips
Chervil can be grown within an herbal garden, whether for culinary or medicinal purposes, but it also works well in an ornamental setting. The delicate, divided leaves are the perfect complement to bold-leaved plants such as cannas, *Colocasia* and hostas.

Recommended
A. cerefolium is an erect-growing annual with scented, deeply divided foliage that appears almost ferny in nature. The white flower clusters emerge on tall stems in summer.

Chervil is best used like parsley, chopped as a garnish or added to salads, soups, sauces, vegetables and meat dishes at the end of cooking. An infusion of the leaves stimulates digestion, relieves head colds, and acts as a blood cleanser.

Features: ornate, useful foliage **Height:** 12–24"
Spread: 10–12" **Hardiness:** treat as an annual

Chives

Allium

The delicate onion flavor of chives is best enjoyed fresh. Mix chives into dips or sprinkle them on salads and baked potatoes.

Growing

Chives grow best in **full sun**. The soil should be **fertile, moist** and **well drained**, but chives adapt to most soil conditions. These plants are easy to start from seed, but they like the soil temperature to stay above 65° F before they will germinate, so seeds started directly in the garden are unlikely to sprout before early summer.

Tips

Chives are decorative enough to be included in a mixed or herbaceous border and can be left to naturalize. In an herb garden, chives should be given plenty of space to allow self-seeding.

Recommended

A. schoenoprasum forms a clump of bright green, cylindrical leaves. Clusters of pinky purple flowers are produced in early and mid-summer. Varieties with white or pink flowers are available.

Chives will spread with reckless abandon as the clumps grow larger and the plants self-seed.

A. schoenoprasum (above & below)

Chives are said to increase appetite and encourage good digestion.

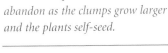

Features: foliage; habit; white, pink, pinky purple flowers **Height:** 8–24" **Spread:** 12" or more **Hardiness:** zones 3–9

Cilantro • Coriander

Coriandrum

C. sativum (above & below)

This plant is a multi-purpose herb. The leaves, called cilantro, can be added to salads, salsas and soups. The seeds, called coriander, are used in pies, chutneys and marmalades.

Growing

Cilantro prefers **full sun** but tolerates partial shade. The soil should be **fertile, light** and **well drained**. These plants dislike humid conditions and grow best during dry summers.

Tips

Cilantro has pungent leaves and is best planted where people will not have to brush past it. It is, however, a delight to behold in flower. Add cilantro plants here and there throughout your borders and vegetable garden. They will create visual appeal and attract pollinators such as bees and butterflies, as well as beneficial insects that deter pest insects.

Recommended

C. sativum forms a clump of lacy basal foliage, similar in appearance to flat-leaf parsley, followed by stalks bearing finely divided leaves and terminating in loose clusters of tiny, white flowers. The seeds ripen in late summer and fall and should be harvested before they shatter.

Features: habit; foliage; white flowers; seeds
Height: 16–24" **Spread:** 8–16"
Hardiness: tender annual

Dill
Anethum

*D*ill leaves and seeds are probably best known for their use as pickling herbs, though they have many other culinary uses.

Growing

Dill grows best in **full sun** in a **sheltered** location out of strong winds. The soil should be of **poor to average fertility, moist** and **well drained**. Sow seeds every couple of weeks in spring and early summer to ensure a regular supply of leaves. Dill should not be grown near fennel because they will cross-pollinate and the seeds of both plants will lose their distinct flavors.

Tips

With its feathery leaves, dill is an attractive addition to a mixed bed or border. It can be included in a vegetable garden but does well in any sunny location. Dill also attracts predatory insects and butterfly caterpillars to the garden.

Recommended

A. graveolens forms a clump of feathery foliage. Clusters of yellow flowers are borne at the tops of sturdy stems in summer. Plants tend to flower early in hot or dry conditions.

Dill turns up frequently in historical records as both a culinary and medicinal herb. It was used by the Egyptians and Romans and is mentioned in the Bible.

A. graveolens (above & below)

Features: feathery, edible foliage; yellow summer flowers; edible seeds
Height: 24–60" **Spread:** 12" or more
Hardiness: annual

Lemon Balm
Melissa

M. officinalis (above & below)

The leaves can be harvested fresh or dried for teas, both hot and cold. They're also useful in flavoring desserts and savory dishes.

This lemon-scented and flavored herb is indispensable to those who love a touch of lemon in most dishes.

Growing
Lemon balm prefers to grow in **full sun** but will grow successfully in locations with dappled shade. The soil should be **moist, fertile** and **well drained** but poor, dry soil is tolerated.

Taking cuttings for use will encourage dense and vigorous growth. It's best to remove the flowers as they emerge.

Tips
Lemon balm is a self-seeder and may spread throughout your garden; it's related to mint, after all. It doesn't possess the same invasive nature, but it may be best to prevent lemon balm from straying.

Herb gardens are often the preferred location for this useful perennial, but it also works well as a fragrant filler in containers, mixed beds and borders.

Recommended
M. officinalis is a bushy, dense-growing perennial with roughly textured, hairy leaves that are fragrant and flavorful when bruised or crushed. Flowers are produced but are considered to be inconspicuous.

Features: fragrant, useful foliage
Height: 24" **Spread:** 18–24"
Hardiness: zones 3–7

Mint

Mentha

The cool, refreshing flavor of mint lends itself to tea and other hot or cold beverages. Mint sauce, made from freshly chopped mint leaves, is often served with lamb.

Growing

Mint grows well in **full sun** or **partial shade**. The soil should be **average to fertile, humus rich** and **moist**. These plants spread vigorously by rhizomes and may need a barrier in the soil to restrict their spread.

Tips

Mint is a good groundcover for damp spots. It grows well along ditches that may only be periodically wet. It also can be used in beds and borders, but place mint carefully because it may overwhelm less vigorous plants.

The flowers attract bees, butterflies and other pollinators to the garden.

Recommended

There are many species, hybrids and cultivars of mint. Spearmint (**M. spicata**), peppermint (**M. x piperita**) and orange mint (**M. x piperita citrata**) are three of the most commonly grown culinary varieties. There are also more decorative varieties with variegated or curly leaves as well as varieties with unusual, fruit-scented leaves.

Three assorted mints with lemon balm (above)
M. x gracilis 'Variegata' (decorative variety, below)

A few sprigs of fresh mint added to a pitcher of iced tea give it an added zip.

Features: fragrant foliage; purple, pink, white summer flowers **Height:** 6–36" **Spread:** 36" or more **Hardiness:** zones 4–8

Oregano • Marjoram
Origanum

O. vulgare 'Polyphant' (above), O. vulgare 'Aureum' (below)

Oregano and marjoram are two of the best known and most frequently used herbs. They are popular in stuffings, soups and stews, and no pizza is complete until it has been sprinkled with fresh or dried oregano leaves.

In Greek, oros *means 'mountain,' and* ganos *means 'joy and beauty,' so oregano translates as 'joy and beauty of the mountain.'*

Growing
Oregano and marjoram grow best in **full sun**. The soil should be of **poor to average fertility, neutral to alkaline** and **well drained**. The flowers attract pollinators to the garden.

Tips
These bushy perennials make a lovely addition to any border and can be trimmed to form low hedges.

Recommended
O. majorana (marjoram) is upright and shrubby with light green, hairy leaves. It bears white or pink flowers in summer and can be grown as an annual where it is not hardy.

O. vulgare **var. hirtum** (oregano, Greek oregano) is the most flavorful culinary variety of oregano. The low, bushy plant has hairy, gray-green leaves and bears white flowers. Many other interesting varieties of *O. vulgare* are available, including those with golden, variegated or curly leaves.

Features: fragrant foliage; white, pink summer flowers; bushy habit **Height:** 12–32" **Spread:** 8–18" **Hardiness:** zones 5–9

Parsley
Petroselinium

Although parsley is usually used as a garnish, it is rich in vitamins and minerals and is reputed to freshen the breath after garlic- or onion-rich foods are eaten.

Growing

Parsley grows well in **full sun** or **partial shade**. The soil should be of **average to rich fertility, humus rich, moist** and **well drained**. Direct sow seeds because the plants resent transplanting. If you start seeds early, use peat pots so the plants can be potted or planted out without disruption.

Tips

Parsley should be started where you mean to grow it as it doesn't transplant well. Containers of parsley can be kept close to the house for easy picking. The bright green leaves and compact growth habit of parsley make it a good edging plant for beds and borders.

P. crispum (above), P. crispum var. crispum (below)

Recommended

P. crispum forms a clump of bright green, divided leaves. This plant is a biennial but is usually grown as an annual because the leaves are the desired parts, not the flowers or the seeds. Cultivars may have flat or curly leaves. Flat leaves are more flavorful and curly are more decorative. Dwarf cultivars are also available.

Parsley leaves make a tasty and nutritious addition to salads. Tear freshly picked leaves and sprinkle them over or mix them in your mixed greens.

Features: attractive foliage **Height:** 8–24"
Spread: 12–24" **Hardiness:** zones 5–8; treat as an annual

Rosemary
Rosmarinus

R. officinalis 'Prostratus' (above), R. officinalis (below)

The needle-like leaves of rosemary are used to flavor a wide variety of culinary dishes, including chicken, pork, lamb, rice, tomato and egg dishes.

Growing

Rosemary prefers **full sun** but tolerates partial shade. The soil should be **well drained** and of **poor to average fertility**.

Tips

Rosemary is often grown in a shrub border or in a container as a specimen or with other plants. Low-growing, spreading plants can be included in a rock garden or along the top of a retaining wall or can be grown in hanging baskets.

Recommended

R. officinalis is a dense, bushy ever-green shrub with narrow, dark green leaves. The habit varies somewhat between cultivars from strongly upright to prostrate and spreading. The flowers are usually in shades of blue, but pink-flowered cultivars are available that can survive in zone 6 in a sheltered location with winter protec-tion. The plants rarely reach their mature size when grown in containers.

To overwinter a container-grown plant, keep it in very light or partial shade outdoors in summer, then put it in a sunny window indoors for winter and keep it well watered but allow it to dry out slightly between waterings.

Features: fragrant, evergreen foliage; bright blue, sometimes pink, summer flowers
Height: 8–48" **Spread:** 12–48"
Hardiness: zones 6–10

Sage
Salvia

Sage is perhaps best known as a flavoring for stuffing, but it has a great range of uses, and is often included in soups, stews, sausages and dumplings.

Growing
Sage prefers **full sun** but tolerates light shade. The soil should be of **average fertility** and **well drained**. These plants benefit from a light mulch of compost each year. They are drought tolerant once established.

Tips
Sage is attractive at the back, in the middle or at the front of a border. Sage can also be grown in mixed planters.

Recommended
S. officinalis is a woody, mounding plant with soft, gray-green leaves. Spikes of light purple flowers appear in early and mid-summer. Many cultivars with attractive foliage are available, including **'Aurea'** (golden sage), bearing chartreuse-yellow leaves touched with dark green markings around the veins; the purple-leaved **'Purpurea'** (purple sage); and the purple, green and cream variegated **'Tricolor,'** which has a pink flush to the new growth.

'Icterina' (above), 'Purpurea' (below)

Sage has been used since at least ancient Greek times as a medicinal and culinary herb and continues to be widely used for both these purposes today.

Features: fragrant, decorative foliage; blue, purple summer flowers **Height:** 12–24"
Spread: 18–36" **Hardiness:** zones 5–8

Summer Savory
Satureia

S. hortensis (left & right)

Savory herbs are often overlooked but are now experiencing a resurgence in popularity. This herb has a strong, peppery, thyme or marjoram-like flavor that is well suited to legume dishes, game meats and patés.

Growing
Summer savory prefers **full sun** in locations with **well-drained, moderately fertile, neutral to slightly alkaline** soils.

For the best flavor, harvest the leaves before the plant flowers. The flavor is known to become bitter after the flowers emerge.

This herb is not tolerant of excessive winter moisture. Prune the older shoots back in early spring.

Summer savory can be grown from seed and directly sown either in early spring or in fall. It can also be started with seedlings and can be propagated with greenwood cuttings.

Tips
Summer savory is not only a useful plant but is also a beautiful annual. It is often planted in herb beds and containers and is the perfect complement to mixed beds and borders as well as rock gardens.

Recommended
S. hortensis is a bushy, aromatic annual that produces narrow, short leaves from the stem base to its tip. Pinkish white to medium pink flowers are produced in summer along the stems, between the leaves.

Features: useful and beautiful flowering annual **Height:** 10–12" **Spread:** 10–12" **Hardiness:** treat as an annual

Sweet Basil
Ocimum

The sweet, fragrant leaves of fresh sweet basil add a delicious, licorice-like flavor to salads and tomato-based dishes.

Growing
Sweet basil grows best in a **warm, sheltered** location in **full sun**. The soil should be **fertile, moist** and **well drained**. Pinch the tips regularly to encourage bushy growth. Plant out or direct sow seed after frost danger has passed in spring.

Tips
Although sweet basil grows best in a warm spot outdoors in the garden, it can be grown successfully indoors in a pot by a bright window to provide you with fresh leaves all year.

Recommended
O. basilicum is one of the most popular of the culinary herbs. There are dozens of varieties, including ones with large or tiny, green or purple and smooth or ruffled leaves.

O. basilicum 'Genovese' and *O. b.* 'Cinnamon' (above)
O. basilicum 'Genovese' (below)

Basil is a good companion plant for tomatoes—both like warm, moist growing conditions and when you pick tomatoes for a salad you'll also remember to include a few sprigs or leaves of basil.

Features: fragrant, decorative leaves
Height: 12–24" **Spread:** 12–18"
Hardiness: tender annual

Thyme

Thymus

T. vulgaris (above), T. x citriodorus (below)

These plants are bee magnets when blooming; thyme honey is pleasantly herbal and goes very well with biscuits.

Thyme is a popular culinary herb used when cooking soups, stews, casseroles and roasts.

Growing

Thyme prefers **full sun**. The soil should be **neutral to alkaline** and of **poor to average fertility**. **Good drainage** is essential. It is beneficial to work leaf mold and sharp limestone gravel into the soil to improve structure and drainage.

Tips

Thyme is useful for sunny, dry locations at the front of borders, between or beside paving stones, on rock gardens and rock walls and in containers.

Once the plants have finished flowering, shear them back by about half to encourage new growth and to prevent the plants from becoming too woody.

Recommended

T. x *citriodorus* (lemon-scented thyme) forms a mound of lemon-scented, dark green foliage. The flowers are pale pink. Cultivars with silver- or gold-margined leaves are available.

T. vulgaris (common thyme) forms a bushy mound of dark green leaves. The flowers may be purple, pink or white. Cultivars with variegated leaves are available.

Features: bushy habit; fragrant, decorative foliage; purple, pink, white flowers **Height:** 8–16" **Spread:** 8–16" **Hardiness:** zones 4–9

Blue Fescue

Festuca

F. glauca 'Elijah Blue' (above), F. glauca (below)

This fine-leaved ornamental grass forms tufted clumps that resemble pincushions. Its metallic blue coloring is an all-season cooling accent for the garden.

Growing

Blue fescue thrives in **full sun to light shade**. The soil should be of **average fertility, moist** and **well drained**. These plants are drought tolerant once established.

Blue fescue emerges early in spring, so shear it back to 1" above the crown in late winter, before new growth emerges. Shear off flower stalks just above the foliage to keep the plant tidy or to prevent self-seeding.

Tips

With its fine texture and distinct blue color, this grass can be used as a single specimen in a rock garden or a container planting. Plant blue fescue in drifts or to edge a bed, border or pathway. It looks attractive in both formal and informal gardens.

Recommended

F. glauca (blue fescue) forms tidy, tufted clumps of fine, blue-toned foliage and panicles of flowers in May and June. Cultivars and hybrids come in varying heights and in shades ranging from blue to olive green. **'Elijah Blue,' 'Boulder Blue,' 'Blue Glow'** and **'Silver Lining'** are popular selections.

Features: blue to blue-green foliage; color that persists into winter; habit **Height:** 6–12" **Spread:** 10–12" **Hardiness:** zones 3–8

Carpet Bugleweed

Ajuga

A. reptans 'Caitlin's Giant' (above & below)

*O*ften labeled as a rampant runner, carpet bugleweed grows best where it can roam freely without competition.

Growing

Carpet bugleweed develops the best leaf color in **partial** or **light shade** but tolerates full shade. The leaves may become scorched when exposed to too much sun. Any **well-drained** soil is suitable.

Divide these vigorous plants any time during the growing season. Remove any new growth or seedlings that don't show the hybrid leaf coloring.

Bugleweed combines well with hostas and ferns; it enjoys the same shady sites and growing conditions.

Tips

Carpet bugleweed is an excellent groundcover for difficult sites, such as exposed slopes or dense shade. It also looks attractive in shrub borders, where its dense growth prevents the spread of all but the most tenacious weeds.

Recommended

A. pyramidalis 'Metallica Crispa' (upright bugleweed) is a very slow-growing plant with metallic bronzy brown, crinkly foliage and violet blue flowers.

A. reptans (carpet bugleweed, common bugleweed) is a low, quick-spreading groundcover. Its many cultivars are often chosen over the species for their colorful, often variegated foliage.

Features: late-spring to early-summer flowers in shades of purple, blue, pink, white; mostly grown for colorful foliage **Height:** 3–12" **Spread:** 6–36" **Hardiness:** zones 3–8

Cinnamon Fern
Osmunda

*F*erns have a certain prehis-
toric mystique and can add
a graceful elegance and textural
accent to the garden.

Growing
Cinnamon ferns prefer **light shade**
but tolerate full sun if the soil is
consistently moist. The soil should
be **fertile, humus rich, acidic** and
moist. Cinnamon ferns tolerate
wet soil and will spread as offsets
form at the plant bases.

Tips
These large ferns form an attractive mass when planted in large
colonies. They can be included in
beds and borders and make a welcome addition to a woodland
garden.

Recommended
O. cinnamomea (cinnamon fern)
has light green fronds that fan out
in a circular fashion from a central
point. Bright green, leafless, fertile
fronds that mature to cinnamon brown
are produced in spring and stand
straight up in the center of the plant.
This species produces 2 ½–5' long
fronds reaching up to the sky.

O. regalis (royal fern) forms a dense
clump of foliage. Feathery, flower-like,
fertile fronds stand out among the sterile
fronds in summer and mature to a rusty
brown. **'Purpurescens'** fronds are purple-red when they emerge in spring and
then mature to green. This contrasts well
with the purple stems.

O. regalis (above), O. cinnamomea (below)

*The flowering fern's 'flowers' are actually its
spore-producing sporangia.*

Features: deciduous, perennial fern; decorative,
fertile fronds; habit **Height:** 2–5' **Spread:** 2–5'
Hardiness: zones 2–8

English Ivy
Hedera

H. helix (above & below)

One of the loveliest things about English ivy is the variation in green and blue tones it adds to the garden.

Growing

English ivy prefers **light shade** or **partial shade** but adapts to any light conditions, from full shade to full sun. The foliage can become damaged or dried out in winter if the plant is grown in a sunny, exposed site. The soil should be of **average to rich fertility, moist** and **well drained**. The richer the soil, the better this vine will grow.

English ivy is a popular houseplant and is frequently used in wire-frame topiaries.

Tips

English ivy is grown as a trailing groundcover that roots at the stem nodes, or as a climbing vine. It clings tenaciously to house walls, tree trunks, stumps and many other rough-textured surfaces. English ivy rootlets can damage walls and fences, and it can be invasive in warmer climates. Choose smaller-leaved cultivars for slower growth.

Recommended

H. helix is a vigorous plant with dark, glossy, triangular, evergreen leaves that may be tinged with bronze or purple in winter, adding another season of interest to your garden. Many cultivars have been developed. Some cultivars have interesting, often variegated foliage. Check with your local garden center to see what is available.

Features: foliage; climbing or trailing habit
Height: 6–8" as a groundcover; up to 90' when climbing **Spread:** indefinite
Hardiness: zones 5–9

Feather Reed Grass

Calamagrostis

This is a graceful, metamorphic grass that changes its habit and flower color throughout the seasons. The slightest breeze keeps this grass in perpetual motion.

Growing

Feather reed grass grows best in **full sun**. The soil should be **fertile, moist** and **well drained**. Heavy clay and dry soils are tolerated. It may be susceptible to rust in cool, wet summers or in sites with poor air circulation. Rain and heavy snow may cause reed grass to flop temporarily, but it quickly bounces back. Cut back the plant to 2–4" in very early spring before growth begins. Divide reed grass if it begins to die out in the center.

Tips

Whether used as a single, stately focal point in small groupings or in large drifts, this is a desirable, low-maintenance grass. It combines well with late-summer and fall-blooming perennials.

Recommended

C. x *acutiflora* 'Karl Foerster' (Foerster's feather reed grass), the most popular selection, forms a loose mound of green foliage from which the airy, distinctly vertical, bottlebrush flowers emerge in June. The flowering stems have a loose, arching habit when they first emerge but grow more stiff and upright over summer. Other cultivars include 'Overdam,' a compact, less hardy selection with white leaf edges. Watch for a new introduction called 'Avalanche,' which has a white center stripe.

'Overdam' (above), 'Karl Foerster' (below)

If you like the way feather reed grass holds its flowers high above its mounded foliage, you might also like Molinia (moor grass) and its species and cultivars. Some have creamy yellow, striped foliage.

Features: open habit; green foliage turns bright gold in fall; winter interest; silvery pink and tan flowerheads **Height:** 3–5'
Spread: 2–3' **Hardiness:** zones 4–9

Fountain Grass
Pennisetum

P. glaucum 'Purple Majesty' (left)
P. setaceum 'Rubrum' (right)

Fountain grass's low maintenance and graceful form make it easy to place. It will soften any landscape, even in winter.

Growing

Fountain grass thrives in **full sun**. The soil should be of **average fertility** and **well drained**. Plants are drought tolerant once established. Plants may self-seed, but are not troublesome. Shear perennials back in early spring and divide them when they start to die out in the center.

Tips

Fountain grass can be used as individual specimen plants, in group plantings and drifts, or combined with flowering annuals, perennials, shrubs and other ornamental grasses. Annual selections

The name Pennisetum alopecuroides *refers to the plumy flower spikes that resemble a fox's tail. In Latin,* penna *means 'feather' and* seta *means 'bristle';* alopekos *is the Greek word for fox.*

are often planted in containers or beds for height and stature.

Recommended

Both perennial and annual fountain grasses exist. Popular perennials include *P. alopecuroides* 'Hameln' (dwarf perennial fountain grass), a compact cultivar with silvery white plumes and narrow, dark green foliage that turns gold in fall (zones 5–8), and *P. orientale* (Oriental fountain grass), with tall, blue-green foliage and large, silvery white flowers (zones 6–8, with winter protection).

Annual fountain grasses include *P. glaucum* **'Purple Majesty'** (purple ornamental millet), which has blackish purple foliage and coarse, bottlebrush flowers. Its form resembles a corn stalk. *P. setaceum* (annual fountain grass) has narrow, green foliage and pinkish purple flowers that mature to gray. Its cultivar, **'Rubrum'** (red annual fountain grass), has broader, deep burgundy foliage and pinkish purple flowers.

Features: arching, fountain-like habit; silvery pink to purplish black foliage; silvery white, pinkish purple flowers; winter interest **Height:** 2–5' **Spread:** 2–3' **Hardiness:** zones 5–9

Japanese Blood Grass

Imperata

Ornamental grasses have so much to offer in a southern landscape, but adding color isn't often one of their unique characteristics. This grass is here to say, bring on the color!

Growing

Japanese blood grass prefers **full to partial sun**, and any soil will do as long as it's **moist** but not wet.

It's important to pull out plants with green blades that emerge from the central clump. Portions that have reverted to green from red will not turn red and have an aggressive to invasive nature.

Tips

Choose a location where the sun will filter through the red leaf blades, so they appear to glow in the garden. Sunny, mixed borders are often best. This grass packs the most punch when planted in uneven groupings.

Recommended

I. cylindrica **'Red Baron'** (*I. cylindrica* var. *rubra*) is a warm-season grass with upright, grassy growth. The blades are somewhat translucent, emerging bright green with red tips. The red intensifies throughout the season, resulting in a deep, wine red by fall. The species *I. cylindrica* is not available in cultivation because of its aggressive and invasive nature. The cultivar will stay put. The foliage continues to change from one stunning color to another, turning to copper in winter.

I. cylindrica 'Red Baron'

Japanese blood grass is also great to brighten up containers, adding a textural element offered by few other plants.

Features: colorful foliage; habit **Height:** 12–18" **Spread:** 12" **Hardiness:** zones 6–9

Japanese Pachysandra
Pachysandra

P. terminalis (above & below)

Low-maintenance Japanese pachysandra is one of the most popular groundcovers. Its rhizomatous rootzone colonizes quickly to form a dense blanket over the ground.

Growing

Japanese pachysandra prefers **light to full shade** but tolerates partial shade. Any soil that is **moist, acidic, humus rich** and **well drained** is good. Plants can be propagated easily from cuttings or by division.

Tips

Japanese pachysandras are durable groundcovers under trees, in shady borders and in woodland gardens. The foliage is considered evergreen, but winter-scorched shoots may need to be removed in spring. Shear or mow old plantings in early spring to rejuvenate them.

Recommended

P. terminalis (Japanese Pachysandra, Japanese Spurge) forms a low mass of foliage rosettes. It grows about 8" tall and can spread almost indefinitely. **'Variegata'** has white margins or mottled silver foliage, but it is not as vigorous as the species. **'Green Sheen'** has, as its name implies, exceptionally glossy leaves that are smaller than those of the species.

Features: perennial, evergreen groundcover; habit; inconspicuous, fragrant, white spring flowers **Height:** 8" **Spread:** 12–18" or more **Hardiness:** zones 3–8

Lady Fern
Athyrium

Lady ferns are striking plants that add a wonderful flair to an otherwise shady, green landscape.

Growing
Lady ferns require **partial shade** in order to maintain their colorful foliage. If they are planted in full shade, the color may not develop, whereas full sun will cause the color to fade or the leaves to scorch. The soil should be **moderately fertile, moist, neutral to acidic** and **humus rich**. Divide in spring when necessary.

It is important to apply a thick layer of mulch in fall to maintain a better moisture level around the roots.

Tips
Lady ferns look very attractive planted en masse in mixed borders or shade gardens and woodland settings.

Recommended
A. felix-femina produces lacy-looking, bright green fronds that form a dense mound of foliage. Cultivars offer different forms, sizes and ornamentation.

A. felix-femina (above & below)

A. felix-femina *is native to most of North America.*

Features: grown for attractive foliage
Height: 4–5' **Spread:** 2–3'
Hardiness: zones 4–9

Maidenhair Fern

Adiantum

A. capillus veneris (above & below)

These charming delicate-looking native ferns add a graceful touch to any woodland planting. Their unique habit and texture will stand out in any garden.

Growing

Maidenhair fern grows well in **light to partial shade** but tolerates full shade. The soil should be of **average fertility, humus rich, slightly acidic** and **moist**. This plant rarely needs dividing, but it can be divided in spring to propagate more plants.

Tips

These lovely ferns do well in any shaded spot in the garden. Include them in rock gardens, woodland gardens, shaded borders and beneath shade trees. They also make an attractive addition to a shaded planting next to a water feature or on a slope where the foliage can be seen when it sways in the breeze.

Recommended

A. capillus veneris (Southern maidenhair) grows 1½' tall and wide, producing triangular, light green fronds. The leaves are fan-shaped in form and are borne along glossy, hair-like, black stems, hence the common name.

Try growing the fine-textured and delicate maidenhair fern with Hostas, Pulmonarias *and* Brunneras. *It will create a nice contrast in texture.*

Features: evergreen, perennial fern; summer and fall foliage; habit **Height:** 12–18" **Spread:** 12–18" **Hardiness:** zones 8–10

Maiden Grass

Miscanthus

One of the most widely grown ornamental grasses available, maiden grass offers vivid colors and ornamental plumes, and needs little maintenance. There is a vast array of species and cultivars to choose from, and most are hardy across our region.

Growing

Maiden grass prefers to grow in **full sun** in **moderately moist**, **fertile**, **well-drained** soil, but it tolerates a variety of conditions.

Tips

Maiden grass creates dramatic impact when massed in a naturalized area or mixed border. Some varieties can grow quite large and are best displayed as specimens. If left standing in fall and winter, the dried foliage and showy plumes look very attractive. Tall varieties make effective temporary summer screens.

Recommended

M. sinsesis is a perennial, clumping grass that spreads slowly from short, thick rhizomes. The many cultivars and hybrids available offer variegated, striped or speckled foliage of one or more colors, and tall, ornate, persistent plumes. **'Gracillimus'** (maiden grass) has long, fine-textured leaves. **'Morning Light'** (variegated maiden grass) is a short and delicate plant with fine, white leaf edges. **'Zebrinus'** (Zebra Grass) produces arching blades with light horizontal stripes from tip to base.

M. sinsesis 'Zebrinus' (above & below)

The fan-shaped plumes are ideal for cutting and for use in crafts, and in fresh or dried arrangements.

Also called: Chinese silver grass, Japanese silver grass, eulalia **Features:** colorful, decorative, strap-like foliage and showy plumes; winter interest **Height:** 3–10' **Spread:** 2–5' **Hardiness:** zones 3–8

Mondo Grass

Ophiopogon

O. planiscapus 'Nigrescens' (above)
O. japonicus 'Bluebird' (below)

Mondo grass is an excellent accent and contrast plant. The foliage of black mondo grass is the perfect black background to highlight any brightly colored plant or flower.

Growing

Mondo grass prefers to grow in **full sun to light shade** in **moist, moderately fertile, well-drained, humus-rich** soil. The foliage is at its best in full sun. Divide in spring just as new growth resumes. These plants appreciate some winter protection of thick mulch in zones 5 and 6.

Tips

Mondo grass can be used as a dense groundcover and for erosion control as it spreads by rhizomes. Use it for border edges and containers. It can be used as a bedding plant in cooler zones, and can be dug up and stored for the winter in a cool, dark room.

Recommended

O. japonicus (mondo grass, monkey grass) produces dark green, grass-like foliage that grows 8–12" long and forms into an evergreen mat of lush foliage, resembling an unkempt lawn. Short spikes or purple flowers emerge in summer, followed by metallic blue fruit. Many cultivars are available in dwarf forms and variegated forms.

O. planiscapus '**Ebknizam**' (EBONY NIGHT) (black mondo grass, black lily turf) has curving, almost black leaves and dark lavender flowers. It grows 4–6" tall and 6–12" wide. '**Nigrescens**' has curving, almost black foliage and pink or white-flushed pink flowers. It grows 6–12" tall and 12" wide. Both cultivars produce blackish, berry-like fruit.

Features: uniquely colored foliage; ground-cover habit; lavender, pink, white-flushed pink flowers **Height:** 4–12" **Spread:** 6–12" **Hardiness:** zones 5–9

Pampas Grass

Cortaderia

C. *selloana* 'Pumila'

This ornamental grass selection requires adequate space to reach its mature size without conflict. Its form and attractive plumes are worth making room for.

C. *selloana* 'Sunningdale Silver'

Growing

Pampas grass prefers to be grown in **full sun** but tolerates light shade. Any kind of soil will do but **fertile, well-drained** soil is best. This plant requires little care once it's planted. Fertilizer and supplemental watering is unnecessary once this grass is established. Division may be necessary however. Pampas grass should be thinned and cut back to a height of 2–3' every spring to keep it from becoming overwhelming.

Tips

Pampas grass is usually integrated into the landscape for its dramatic flower plumes that last until they're cut down in spring. They're effective windbreaks when planted in groups but only when space allows. Pampas grass is the perfect coastal plant and can tolerate dry slopes.

Do not plant this stunner too close to walkways, patios or places with moderate to heavy foot traffic; the edge of each blade is razor sharp.

Recommended

C. selloana is the true pampas grass, unlike other too-weedy species that are often sold by the same name. This species produces sharply edged, grayish green leaves and tall, fluffy flower plumes in shades of tan. The species grows approximately 8–10' tall and 5–6' wide. Cultivars are available with variegated foliage and in dwarf forms.

Features: habit; tan flower plumes
Height: 4–10' **Spread:** 4–10'
Hardiness: zones 8–10

Strawberry Geranium
Saxifraga

S. stolonifera 'Kinki Purple' (above), S. stolonifera (below)

This perennial groundcover is neither a begonia nor a geranium but displays physical characteristics reminiscent of both.

There are more than 400 species of *Saxifraga* and even more cultivars, but the strawberry begonia or *S. stolonifera* is probably one of the best selections for the South for all it has to offer and for its tolerance to excessive heat.

Growing

Strawberry geranium prefers to be planted in **partial to full shade**. The soil should be **neutral to alkaline, fertile, moist** and **well drained**. Divide in spring.

Tips

Strawberry geranium is an excellent addition to rock gardens and borders but also works well in shaded, mixed borders. It is a beautiful addition to hanging baskets and can also be used as a groundcover in moist soil.

Recommended

S. stolonifera (strawberry geranium, strawberry begonia, mother of thousands) produces a thick, semi-evergreen mat of attractive, gray-veined leaves with purple undersides, and tiny, white flowers borne on spikes. The parent plant sends out shoots at the end of which grow tiny new plants.

Features: white summer flowers; attractive foliage; spreading habit **Height:** 1–2'
Spread: 2' **Hardiness:** zones 7–9

Vinca
Vinca

Vinca is a dependable, spreading ground-cover, and one plant can cover almost any size area. Its reliability is second to none, and its ease of growth is sure to please.

Growing
Vinca grows best in **partial to full shade** in **moist, fertile, well-drained** soil. It adapts to many types of soil but turns yellow if the soil is too dry or the sun is too hot. Divide in early spring or fall, or whenever it becomes overgrown.

Tips
Vinca is a useful and attractive groundcover in a shrub border, under trees or on a shady bank, and it prevents soil erosion. It is shallow-rooted and able to out-compete weeds but won't interfere with deeper-rooted shrubs.

If vinca begins to outgrow its space, shear it back hard in early spring. The sheared-off ends may have rooted along the stems. These rooted cuttings may be potted and given away as gifts, or may be introduced to new areas of the garden.

V. minor (above & below)

Recommended
V. major forms a mat of vigorous, upright to trailing stems bearing dark green, evergreen foliage. Purple to violet blue flowers are borne in a flush in spring and sporadically throughout summer. **'Variegata'** has creamy white-edged foliage.

V. minor (lesser periwinkle) forms a low, loose mat of trailing stems. Purple or blue flowers are borne in a flush in spring and sporadically all summer. **'Alba'** bears white flowers.

Vinca is a great plant for use in mixed containers. As it drapes over the container edge, it dramatically enhances its companions.

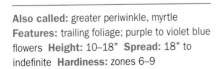

Also called: greater periwinkle, myrtle
Features: trailing foliage; purple to violet blue flowers **Height:** 10–18" **Spread:** 18" to indefinite **Hardiness:** zones 6–9

Wintercreeper Euonymus

Euonymus

E. fortunei 'Emerald 'n' Gold' (above & below)

This evergreen vine can also be grown as a shrub.

This evergreen creeper is well suited for use as a groundcover and will act as a living mulch around shrubs in mixed borders and beds.

Growing

Wintercreeper euonymus prefers **full sun** but tolerates light or partial shade. Soil of **average to rich fertility** is preferable but any **moist, well-drained** soil will do.

Tips

Wintercreeper euonymus can be grown as a climber with support, or left to trail along the ground as a groundcover.

Recommended

E. fortunei is rarely grown as a species owing to the wide and attractive variety of cultivars. These can be prostrate, climbing or mounding evergreens, often with attractive, variegated foliage. **'Gracilis'** and **'Harlequin'** are cultivars noted for their colorful, variegated foliage. **'Coloratus'** produces dark green foliage that turns reddish purple in fall when the temperatures cool off.

Features: deciduous or evergreen ground-cover or climber; attractive foliage
Height: 24" **Spread:** indefinite
Hardiness: zones 3–9

Glossary

Acid soil: soil with a pH lower than 7.0

Annual: a plant that germinates, flowers, sets seed and dies in one growing season

Alkaline soil: soil with a pH higher than 7.0

Basal leaves: leaves that form from the crown, at the base of the plant

Bract: a modified leaf at the base of a flower or flower cluster

Corm: a bulb-like, food-storing, underground stem, resembling a bulb without scales

Crown: the part of the plant at or just below soil level where the shoots join the roots

Cultivar: a cultivated plant variety with one or more distinct differences from the species, e.g., in flower color or disease resistance

Damping off: fungal disease causing seedlings to rot at soil level and topple over

Deadhead: to remove spent flowers to maintain a neat appearance and encourage a longer blooming season

Direct sow: to sow seeds directly in the garden

Dormancy: a period of plant inactivity, usually during winter or unfavorable conditions

Double flower: a flower with an unusually large number of petals

Genus: a category of biological classification between the species and family levels; the first word in a scientific name indicates the genus

Grafting: a type of propagation in which a stem or bud of one plant is joined onto the rootstock of another plant of a closely related species

Hardy: capable of surviving unfavorable conditions, such as cold weather or frost, without protection

Hip: the fruit of a rose, containing the seeds

Humus: decomposed or decomposing organic material in the soil

Hybrid: a plant resulting from natural or human-induced cross-breeding between varieties, species or genera

Inflorescence: a flower cluster

Male clone: a plant that may or may not produce pollen but that will not produce fruit, seed or seedpods

Neutral soil: soil with a pH of 7.0

Perennial: a plant that takes three or more years to complete its life cycle

pH: a measure of acidity or alkalinity; the soil pH influences availability of nutrients for plants

Rhizome: a root-like, food-storing stem that grows horizontally at or just below soil level, from which new shoots may emerge

Rootball: the root mass and surrounding soil of a plant

Seedhead: dried, inedible fruit that contains seeds; the fruiting stage of the inflorescence

Self-seeding: reproducing by means of seeds without human assistance, so that new plants constantly replace those that die

Semi-double flower: a flower with petals in two or three rings

Single flower: a flower with a single ring of typically four or five petals

Species: the fundamental unit of biological classification; the entity from which cultivars and varieties are derived

Standard: a shrub or small tree grown with an erect main stem, accomplished either through pruning and training or by grafting the plant onto a tall, straight stock

Sucker: a shoot that comes up from the root, often some distance from the plant; it can be separated to form a new plant once it develops its own roots

Tender: incapable of surviving the climatic conditions of a given region and requiring protection from frost or cold

Tuber: the thick section of a rhizome bearing nodes and buds

Variegation: foliage that has more than one color, often patched or striped or bearing leaf margins of a different color

Variety: a naturally occurring variant of a species

Index of Recommended Plant Names

Bold indicates main plant entries; *italics* indicate botanic name.

Author Biographies

Richard Nunnally holds a bachelor's and a master's degree from Virginia Commonwealth University and began his career with Virginia Cooperative Extension in 1968. He served as an agricultural extension agent, specializing in environmental horticulture, until his retirement from Virginia Tech in July, 2002. Over the course of his career with Cooperative Extension, Richard received numerous state and national awards for his work in public information. In April, 1998, he was awarded the prestigious Alumni Award of Excellence in Extension at Virginia Tech's Founders' Day ceremony. Richard has been host of *Virginia Home Grown*, a monthly TV show on PBS carried throughout central Virginia, since its inception in 2001. He also writes a weekly gardening column for the *Richmond Times Dispatch*, and is an adjunct instructor at J. Sergeant Reynolds Community College.

Laura Peters is a certified Master Gardener with 17 gardening books to her credit. She has gained valuable experience in every aspect of the horticultural industry in a career that has spanned more than 18 years. She enjoys sharing her practical knowledge of organic gardening, plant varieties and gardening products with fellow gardeners.

Acknowledgments

I am extremely grateful to the many extension specialists, extension agents, master gardeners, and others in the horticulture industry throughout Virginia who taught, supported and otherwise influenced me over the years. I wish to particularly thank Stacey Arnold, Amy Barton, Annette Critelli, Doug Hensel, Mark Landa and especially my wife, Susan, for her patience and support during the past 37 years. *Richard Nunnally*

A big thanks to my parents, Gary and Lucy Peters and my friends for their endless encouragement and support all these years. I would also like to thank Richard Nunnally for his enthusiasm, valuable expertise and assistance. The following people and places embraced this project and did everything in their power to assist me in my travels and to answer all of my questions. Thanks to the J.C. Raulston Arboretum, the North Carolina Botanical Garden at the University of NC at Chapel Hill, Brock Chisholm and The New Hanover County Arboretum in Wilmington, Linda Lawson, Jim McDaniel and Airlie Gardens, Tony Avent, the Plant Delights Nursery & the Juniper Level Botanic Gardens, Raleigh Little Theater Rose Garden, Garden Supply Company and the Gardens for the Cure garden tour, Stefany and Jay Rhodes and the Front Street Inn and last but not least, Darlene and Kevin Smith. Thanks to those who allowed me to photograph their gardens, pick their brains and use their fabulous images, including Blair Durant of Niche Gardens and Jackson and Perkins. *Laura Peters*